W9-CYE-607

Home Remodeling: Floors & Ceilings

Paul Currie

Handyman Club Library™

Handyman Club of America
Minneapolis, Minnesota

Home Remodeling: Floors & Ceilings

By Paul Currie

CREDITS

Mike Vail
Vice President, New Product & Business Development

Tom Carpenter
Director of Books & New Media Development

Mark Johanson
Book Products Development Manager, Editor

Dan Cary
Photo Production Coordinator

Chris Marshall
Editorial Coordinator

Steve Anderson
Senior Editorial Assistant

Paul Currie
Author

Bill Nelson
Series Design, Art Direction and Production

Mark Macemon, Ralph Karlen
Photography

Jon Hegge, John Nadeau
Builders

Mario Ferro
Illustrator

Blake Stranz
Contributing Writer

Scott Jacobson
Contributing Photographer

Brad Classon
Production Assistance

Jason Menk
Wood Flooring Consultant

Dan Kennedy
Book Production Manager

ISBN 1-58159-085-7

Handyman Club of America
12301 Whitewater Drive
Minnetonka, Minnesota 55343

Table of Contents

Introduction

Floors and ceilings set the tone of a room. If your floor is in disrepair or covered with a floorcovering that's woefully outdated, you can remodel every other element of the room with the finest materials known to man and the overall impression of the room will still be that it is old or rundown. The same holds true for the ceiling, although to a lesser extent.

Depending on which materials you choose to use and the pre-existing condition of the floor or ceiling, remodeling these parts of a room can be a very simple and inexpensive process. In fact, many of the most popular (and do-it-yourself friendly) flooring products can be installed in a single weekend, or even a single day.

In *Home Remodeling: Floors & Ceilings,* produced by the Handyman Club of America exclusively for its Members, you'll find comprehensive information on the most popular floor and ceiling remodeling projects. Installing "floating floor" systems, laying hardwood strip flooring, laying tile (both ceramic and vinyl), installing sheet vinyl and refinishing wood floors are just a few of the topics covered in the flooring section of the book. Along with these subjects, you'll find clear, useful instructions on reviving a ceiling with projects such as hanging suspended ceilings and installing embossed metal panels. You'll also find an extremely thorough treatment that shows you the ins and outs of one of the most dreaded home improvement projects: installing wallboard on a ceiling.

In addition to the information on new installations, you'll also encounter many helpful hints and step-by-step sequences for repairing floor and ceiling materials. And to round out the treatment, we've included special sections on attaching trim and molding to floors and ceilings.

Remodeling a floor or ceiling is not just an exercise in keeping current with new design trends (although it's certainly possible to approach it that way). It is a way to make your home more comfortable and attractive—to you and your family as well as to prospective buyers.

The best time to undertake a floor or ceiling remodeling project is during a wall-to-wall, all-out remodeling project. As a general rule of thumb, most remodelers prefer to install the floorcoverings last so the new products aren't damaged while other work is being done. If you're considering replacing base cabinets or bathroom fixtures, you have an excellent opportunity to update your floor and ceiling. But the beauty of these independent projects is that you can do them just about any time you like.

Take a close look at your floors and ceilings. Imagine that your sunsplash pattern, sticky-back vinyl flooring is gone and in its place is a beautiful wood floor with a gleaming, hard-as-rock factory finish. Inspect the peeling paint and the crumbling plaster on your ceiling. Now picture a romantic, nostalgic pressed metal ceiling above your head instead. The difference can be astounding, and the possibilities are practically endless.

Gallery of Ideas

From hardwood strip flooring to porcelain tile to resilient sheet vinyl, the world of flooring is vast and growing all the time. To help you begin the decision-making process for your next floor remodeling project, the photos on the following pages show a small sampling of the most common floorcovering products on the market today. And just in case all this flooring discussion is a little over your head, we've included some photos of ceiling possibilities. The number of products and options is more limited with ceilings than with floors, but the impact of a fabulous ceiling project can be stunning.

(right) *Combining multiple layout approaches creates an interesting and sophisticated appearance with basic ceramic tile.*

Dal Tile

Mannington

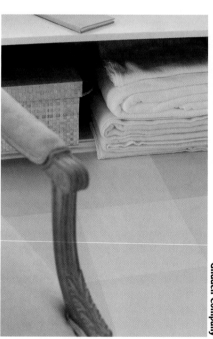

Glidden Company

Slight variations in tone give the painted checkerboard design on this bathroom floor a sense of warmth and activity.

The appearance of multiple glazes and a pattern of 6-in.-square tiles with diamond insets give this resilient sheet flooring the look of expensive ceramic tile.

Exotic wood grain and tones in this laminated flooring are a testament to how advanced the manufacturers of engineered wood flooring products have become.

Mannington

Acoustical tile panels are scored to create the look of smaller ceiling tiles while preserving the ease of installation of 2 × 4 ft. panels.

(right) Paint is a traditional treatment for porch floors, but this porch goes well beyond the ubiquitous battleship gray, creating a fun and relaxing impression with a subdued rainbow effect.

Glidden Company

The inspiration for this knotty heart pine laminate flooring design came from actual floorboards salvaged from an automobile factory in Indiana.

Traditionally, resilient sheet flooring has muted tones and a subtle, often geometric pattern that blends into just about any decorating scheme.

The rich colors and patterns of Brazilian cherry are replicated very effectively in this laminate flooring.

Strips of wood molding are used to conceal the drop-down light fixture bases and link this acoustical tile ceiling visually with walls and trim in the rest of this room.

American Olean

10-in. octagonal tiles are combined with dark accent squares to display a cheerful attitude.

Three different sizes (6 × 6, 6 × 12, and 12 × 12 in.) are intertwined cleverly in the field of this ceramic tile installation.

Dal Tile

Tumbled marble is yet another effect that can be created with ceramic tile (and at a fraction of the cost of the real material).

Glazed ceramic tiles replicate the appearance and texture of granite. The effect is enhanced by the two-tone checkerboard layout pattern.

A perimeter row of decorative accent tiles establishes the borders in this kitchen floor, and is repeated to frame the island.

A permanent area rug is added to this dining room by fitting decorative parquet tiles into the layout of this wood strip floor. Switching to a herringbone pattern in the field area of the "rug" contributes to the illusion.

The look of stone tile lends rustic appeal to this soft, contemporary room.

American Olean

Shanker Industries

Resilient sheet vinyl can offer the texture and appearance of just about any tile, including the mosaic pattern here. Yet it's easy to install and warm underfoot.

(left) Embossed metal ceiling panels were once the standard in public buildings and finer homes. Today, their romantic appeal is causing a comeback in their popularity.

Old-world charm that rivals the appeal of antique wood can be achieved with ceramic tile when put into the right setting.

A wide expanse of floor can be installed economically and without sacrificing style using resilient sheet vinyl.

Wood floors add warmth and beauty to any room, whether they're genuine wood or a cunning approximation.

(above) Mixing materials offers a wealth of interesting design options, as demonstrated by this unique blend of hardwood, decorative parquet and marble tile.

(right) Successful ceilings often blend into the background, letting the other elements of the room grab most of the attention.

Mannington

USG Corporation

FLOORING PROJECTS

Floor Remodeling Projects

**Painted Floors
(Pages 98 to 103)**

**Ceramic Tile Floors
(Pages 26 to 45)**

**Refinishing Floors
(Pages 66 to 71)**

Wood Floors (Pages 46 to 65)

Resilient Flooring (Pages 76 to 91)

Carpeting (Pages 92 to 97)

Floor remodeling projects are among the most friendly do-it-yourself endeavors, largely because so many of the products are designed especially for use by weekenders.

Flooring Basics

Few remodeling projects can provide a greater return for a minimal investment of time and money than floor remodeling projects. Depending on the type of floorcovering you choose, you can give any room a fresh new look in a single weekend: A decorative paint treatment or a new surface of self-adhesive vinyl tiles or foam-back carpet are just three examples of quick-and-easy floor remodeling projects that won't break your back or your bank account. But if your tastes run a little more toward the high end, there are plenty of top-of-the-line floorcovering projects that will add character, richness and individuality to your home.

Installing ceramic or natural stone tile or wood flooring generally takes more time and money, but these projects remain among the most popular floor remodeling approaches.

If you are remodeling an existing kitchen or bathroom, remove base cabinets and vanities if possible. Installation of the underlayment will be easier and you won't 'lock in' the cabinets (which can cause problems if you want to replace cabinets at a future date). Also remove any floor-mounted fixtures, like toilets or floor-standing appliances. If you are replacing the tub or shower in the bathroom, this should be done before installing underlayment. You will also need to remove the trim molding around the floor.

In most cases, it makes more sense to remove the underlayment along with the floorcovering. Set your circular saw to cut through both layers (usually, a ½-in. cutting depth will work), then cut the floorcovering and underlayment into manageable strips and pry them away from the subfloor.

Removing old floorcoverings

Plan on removing old floorcoverings before installing a new floorcovering. If the old floorcovering is thin resilient tile or sheet vinyl that's in good condition, you may be able to install new vinyl floorcovering products directly on top of the old floorcovering. But generally, this practice is not recommended—the old floorcovering may be concealing damaged underlayment or even a moisture problem. Most floorcoverings are installed over a layer of underlayment—usually ¼-in. plywood. Especially if the floorcovering has been fully bonded to the underlayment, you'll be better off removing the old underlayment along with the old floorcovering.

NOTE: Linoleum and resilient tiles installed before the 1970s may contain asbestos and, if so, should be treated as a hazardous material. Before removing older linoleum, bring a sample to your local waste disposal authority for testing, and follow all recommendations and local regulations for removal and disposal.

REMOVING RESILIENT FLOORING AND LINOLEUM

Cut the floorcovering and underlayment into strips about 2 ft. wide, using a circular saw set to about ½-in. cutting depth (See photo, top of page). Finish the cut with a reciprocating saw or hand saw, then pull the strips away from the subfloor with a pry bar.

OPTION: If the old floorcovering was bonded to a subfloor, concrete floor or hardwood floor, slice it into strips with a utility knife and peel the strips off as best you can. Remove remaining material and adhesive with a long-handled floor scraper. Soak stubborn adhesives with warm, soapy water.

HOW TO REMOVE OLD CERAMIC TILE

From subfloor or concrete floor: Use a cold chisel and maul to chip off old ceramic tiles. Always direct the blow away from your body and away from any floor drains, pipes or other obstructions. Use a long-handled scraper to remove old mortar if you're unable to remove the underlayment. Wear eye protection and gloves.

From floor underlayment: Chisel a pathway in ceramic tile floors to create clearance for your circular saw. Then, cut through the underlayment and remove the old floor in sections. It is possible to cut through the ceramic tile with a circular saw and masonry blade, but it generates a high volume of fine dust you're better off avoiding.

Working Safely

Protective equipment is critical to a safe and successful home remodeling project. Wear a respirator (A) whenever working with dangerous chemicals or very fine dust; safety glasses (B) or goggles (C) shield your eyes whenever operating power tools or performing any potentially dangerous activity—even striking a nail with a hammer; wear hearing protection (D) when operating power tools; a particle mask (E) prevents you from breathing in dust; and work gloves (F) should be worn whenever handling building materials.

Safety tip: One of the greatest hazards you'll encounter when remodeling floors and ceilings is waste and clutter from removing old materials. Dispose of all remodeling waste immediately.

Subfloors & Underlayment

Without proper subfloor and underlayment materials that are flat, stable and in good condition, your flooring projects are at risk—despite the high quality of materials or installation techniques you use. Even minor underlayment imperfections may show through resilient flooring, and cracked grout lines between ceramic floor tiles are almost guaranteed if there is too much give to the floor beneath.

A solid and level subfloor is the beginning of all successful flooring projects. It supports the underlayment and the finished flooring materials. Subflooring is usually made of ¾-in.-thick plywood, although many homes built before the 1950s have subfloors made of pine boards installed on the diagonal across the floor joists. This material must be in good condition; any damaged or low areas must be repaired before underlayment or flooring materials are installed.

Once you have removed old flooring materials and underlayment, examine the subflooring carefully. If you need to remove flooring or underlayment because of water damage or dry rot, be certain you also check the subfloor for any damage. Before repairing subflooring, make certain you have determined the cause of the damage and fixed the problem, otherwise the damage will reoccur. Also look for damaged joists underneath the repair area—if you find rot or other structural weakness, have a professional contractor repair the joists.

When making subflooring repairs, you may need to shim because of differences in thickness between old subflooring materials and new plywood (which often isn't truly ¾ in. thick).

The purpose of flooring underlayment is to provide a smooth, stable substrate for floorcoverings. Cementboard (shown here) is used to create a base for tile installations, especially in wet areas. Plywood, generally ¼ in. thick, is used for most other underlayment installations. Use either exterior-grade or lauan plywood (See photo, below right).

Subfloor inspection

An uneven subfloor will affect your ability to create a smooth underlayment surface. This can cause difficulty in installing new flooring. It also can cause uneven wear or early deterioration of the flooring. Frequently, one or more sagging floor joists are the cause of an uneven subfloor. To determine if your subfloor is flat, lay a straightedge that's at least 4 ft. long across the floor in different spots. Dips no deeper than ¼ in. and no wider than 2 ft. (caused by one slightly sagging joist) can be filled with floor leveler compound. More significant dips indicate more serious joist problems and should be examined by a professional contractor.

Also check for sloping subfloors. Minor slopes (less than ½ in. over 12 ft.) are not unusual and generally are not a problem. Slopes greater than this may indicate a serious foundation or other structural problem and should also be examined by a professional.

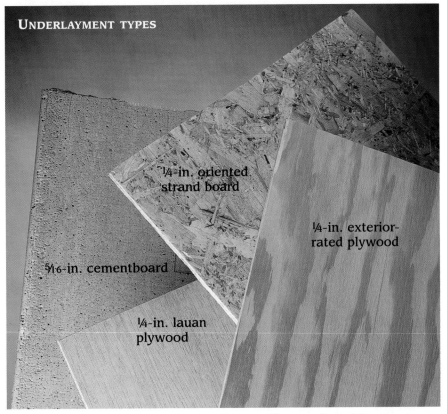

UNDERLAYMENT TYPES

¼-in. oriented strand board

⁵⁄₁₆-in. cementboard

¼-in. exterior-rated plywood

¼-in. lauan plywood

Choose floor underlayment material based on the type of floor covering and the general exposure to moisture. For bathroom installations, use exterior-rated plywood (BC) as an underlayment, except when laying ceramic floor tile, which requires a cementboard underlayment. In drier areas, you can save a little money by using oriented strand board or lauan plywood, but only with certain types of sheet flooring.

Repairing subfloors

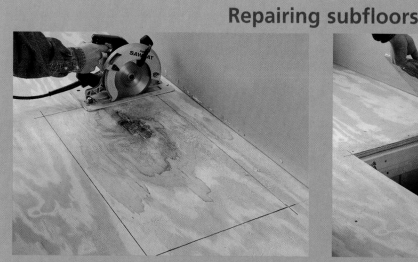

One of the best reasons to remove old floorcoverings and underlayment (instead of installing new materials over them) is that it gives you a chance to inspect your subfloor and floor joists. With early detection, you can stave off the need to remove a perfectly good floor to attend to a problem later on if it becomes more severe. If you find rot in your subfloor, the first thing you need to do is determine the source of the moisture—usually a leaky pipe or a bad seal around a toilet, shower or bathtub. Once you have corrected the problem, repair the subfloor. If the damaged area is relatively small, cut it out with a circular saw (left photo). A circular saw set to the thickness of the subfloor is a safer tool to use than a reciprocating saw, which may cut through plumbing lines or wiring. If more than half of the subfloor sheathing sheet is damaged, simply remove the entire sheet. Try to locate cuts so they're centered over joists. Remove the bad area, inspect the joists to make sure they're not damaged, then cut a patch from exterior plywood the same thickness as the original subfloor and test the fit (right photo). The patch should be about ¼ in. smaller than the opening in both directions. Secure to the floor joists with deck screws. If the floor joists are showing signs of damage or rot, contact your local building department for advice.

Subfloors

Wood flooring and carpet are usually installed directly over the subfloor. Since these materials are more flexible, the additional layer of plywood or cementboard is not required. Seams and small imperfections in the subflooring surface are acceptable. However, the subfloor must be flat and in good condition to provide proper support for these flooring materials. Resin paper or 15-pound building paper (See page 51) can be installed underneath nailed-down floors to help prevent squeaking.

A concrete slab that is smooth and stable provides adequate support for ceramic tile and other glued-down flooring materials. Dips and minor unevenness can be filled with floor leveler compound. Cracks should be covered with isolation membrane (See photo, next page, lower left). It is best to float an engineered-wood floor over concrete so a moisture barrier can be installed. A nailed-down wood floor generally is not practical over concrete because it requires the extra cost and floor height of an additional plywood subfloor laid over the concrete.

Underlayment

Underlayment that is smooth and stable is vital for the durability and attractiveness of most flooring materials. A flat underlayment without seams, gaps or ridges is a must for vinyl floors. Underlayment for tile and stone floors can have small gaps or seams and be rougher in texture, but must be level and without ridges. This underlayment must also be rigid—any give to the floor will result in cracking or loosened tiles.

Some new flooring materials can be installed over existing flooring (check where you purchase flooring materials for product recommendations), but the existing flooring must be tightly bonded to the underlayment to make this successful. Also keep in mind the additional floor height this method will cause.

Otherwise, plan on removing existing floor coverings and, in most cases, the underlayment as well (it's usually easier to get the old flooring up this way). Always replace the underlayment if it is not in good condition. You should suspect underlayment damage if the existing flooring is loose or stained from water damage, as is often a problem in bathrooms. Once the floorcovering is removed, clean the surface of the underlayment. Check for damaged areas. Soft or swollen underlayment must be replaced. If you've removed vinyl flooring, all of the backing and glue must be removed from the underlayment. Any grout or adhesive remaining from a tile floor must also be removed. Or you can install another layer of underlayment over the old if this won't cause clearance problems when the finished floor surface is in place.

Using floor leveler products

Subfloor

Various types of floor leveler products are used to fill small irregularities in concrete, subfloor or underlayment surfaces. Some, called embossing levelers, are spread over existing flooring such as tile or vinyl, allowing installation of new flooring without removal of the old (left photo). Floor levelers usually come as a dry mixture that is combined with a latex or acrylic additive, but premixed products are available. Spread floor leveler compound to fill low spots or feather out uneven areas. Apply several thin layers of leveler rather than one thick one (right photo). Check with a straightedge to make certain the floor leveler is flat and level with the surrounding subfloor. Apply more leveler if necessary. Let dry and sand smooth.

Isolation membrane: a solution for tiling over cracked concrete floors

Isolation membrane protects tile flooring from the independent movement between areas of a cracked concrete subfloor. If there are only a few cracks, cut strips of membrane wide enough to cover the crack by several inches on either side. Spread the adhesive recommended by the manufacturer (often thin-set mortar) over the crack area, then press and flatten the membrane into the adhesive. Install isolation membrane over the entire floor when there are many cracks. Cut sheets of membrane several inches longer than the room width. Spread adhesive for one sheet at a time, then embed the membrane in the adhesive. Use a flooring roller to flatten the membrane, then trim it flush with the walls using a straightedge and utility knife. You may need to roll and trim a few times to remove all ridges from the membrane. Make certain to butt the seams of adjoining sheets without any overlap.

Plywood underlayment

Use quality-grade plywood for underlayment. Exterior-rated plywood should be used underneath vinyl flooring in areas where moisture is an issue, such as kitchens and bathrooms. High-quality lauan or other interior rated plywood can be used in drier areas. Particleboard can be installed as an underlayment for carpet, if needed. Always follow the flooring manufacturer's requirements for underlayment or your product warranty may be voided.

Plan the underlayment installation so there will be as few seams as possible, and so the long edges of the plywood sheets will be screwed into joists, not just the subflooring. Underlayment seams should be staggered from those of the subfloor. Extra time spent here will save a great deal of effort later in making a smooth, stable surface, particularly for vinyl flooring.

1 Remove base moldings, vent covers and other obstacles that can be taken off the floor area, such as toilets. Installing new underlayment is easiest without base cabinets in place, which is why a flooring project is a great time to plan on replacing cabinets. Check the condition of the subfloor and make repairs as needed (See page 21). Clean the subfloor thoroughly. Any dirt or other debris caught between subflooring and underlayment can cause noise or flooring failure in the future. Cut and install each piece of the underlayment using screws long enough to penetrate into the joists. Drive screws every 6 in. at the edges of the underlayment pieces, and every 12 in. in the field, but keep screws at least ½ in. from the edge of the plywood. Drive screw heads just below the surface of the underlayment. Leave a ⅛-in. gap between pieces and a ½-in. gap along walls to allow for expansion.

2 Fill seams and screw head dimples with floor leveler compound, following manufacturer's directions for mixing and applying the compound. Feather the edges as much as possible. Note: If you are installing plywood underlayment for ceramic tile, use the same thin set mortar used for the tile to do this. After the compound has dried thoroughly, sand smooth with a random orbit sander, using 100 or 120 grit sandpaper. Be careful to sand evenly and only as much as necessary so you don't create a low spot.

3 Check for low spots using a straightedge. Reapply compound and sand as necessary. Clean floor thoroughly before installing flooring material.

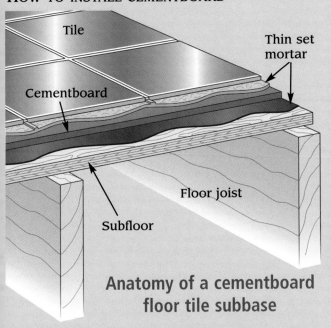

Tile

Thin set
mortar

Cementboard

Floor joist

Subfloor

Anatomy of a cementboard floor tile subbase

The most stable underlayment for ceramic tile flooring is cement-board (also known as concrete backerboard). Cementboard underlay-ment for floor tile installations is bonded to a sturdy subfloor with thin-set mortar. The seams and screw heads should be taped and filled with thin-set. Then, the tile can be set into a mortar bed applied over the cementboard.

Carbide blade
cutter

1 Plan the layout for cementboard just as for plywood underlay-ment. Cut cementboard to size using the score-and-snap method of cutting wallboard, except use a carbide-blade cutter rather than a utility knife (See page 119 for a demonstration of the score-and-snap technique for cutting sheet goods). Use a wallboard T-square as a straightedge for marking and cutting.

2 Spread a layer of thin-set mortar on the subfloor before attach-ing cementboard sheets, using a ¼-in. notched trowel. Drive deck screws (long enough to penetrate the joists) every 8 in. at the edges, keeping screws at least ½ in. from edges. Drill pilot holes to make this easier. Leave a ⅛-in. gap between sheets and a ½-in. gap along walls. Drive shorter deck screws at 8 in. intervals in the field.

3 Fill the gaps between sheets with thin-set mortar, then embed fiberglass joint tape into the thin-set. Spread more mortar over the tape and smooth it out in as thin a layer as possible. After the mortar has dried thoroughly, strike off any rough ridges with a putty knife.

A ceramic or stone tile floor has many advantages over other types of floors. Tile is perhaps the most durable floorcovering; it is easy to clean; it resists moisture; and it creates a rich, beautiful image for your room.

Ceramic & Stone Tile

The beauty of a ceramic or stone tile floor is timeless. Solid-color tiles come in a rainbow of color options with many textures. There also are printed and hand-painted ceramic tiles used as accent tiles. You aren't limited to square shapes; there are rectangular, round, hexagonal and irregular shapes. Depending on your taste and room use, tile shapes, colors and textures can be combined into a stunning floor. Ceramic and stone tiles are the hardest floor surface and can be very expensive. But a tile floor is durable and retains its looks almost forever if properly maintained.

When planning a new tile floor in a kitchen or bathroom, it's also a great time to consider replacing cabinets and countertops and making other changes. Installing tile is much faster with cabinets removed since you won't have to trim tile to fit around them. Also, installing new cabinets on the tile floor is much easier than fitting them into the recessed outline of the previous cabinets. The toilet must be removed when installing new tile. With cabinets, countertops and sinks out of the way, there will never be an easier time to replace the bathtub or shower.

Tile Types

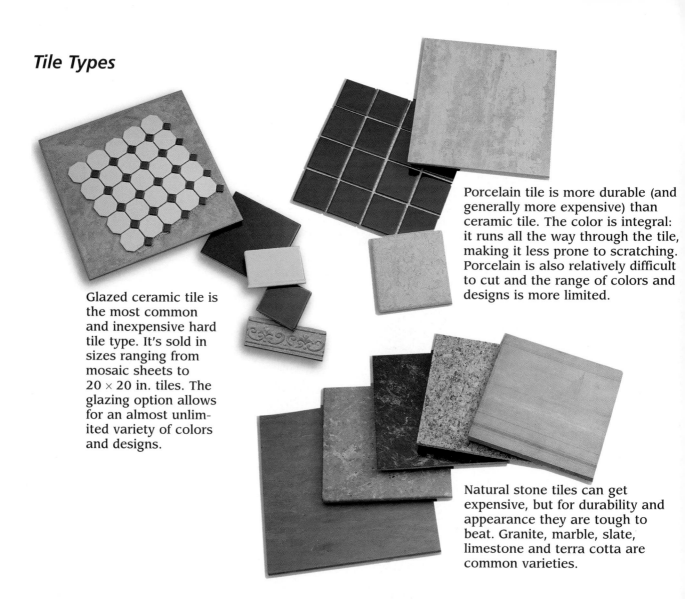

Glazed ceramic tile is the most common and inexpensive hard tile type. It's sold in sizes ranging from mosaic sheets to 20 × 20 in. tiles. The glazing option allows for an almost unlimited variety of colors and designs.

Porcelain tile is more durable (and generally more expensive) than ceramic tile. The color is integral: it runs all the way through the tile, making it less prone to scratching. Porcelain is also relatively difficult to cut and the range of colors and designs is more limited.

Natural stone tiles can get expensive, but for durability and appearance they are tough to beat. Granite, marble, slate, limestone and terra cotta are common varieties.

Pattern options

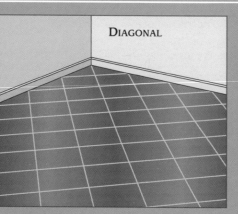

DIAGONAL

RUNNING BOND

DIAGONAL: In a perfectly square room, diagonal lines marked from corner to corner are usable reference lines (just make certain they are perpendicular). Otherwise, mark perpendicular reference lines in the most visible floor area (steps 1 through 3 of the standard floor tile layout, pages 30 to 31). Mark another reference line at a 45° angle to these lines, through their intersection. You can use the 3-4-5 right triangle method for marking perpendicular lines for this, too—both angles opposite the right 90° angle are 45° angles. After making this diagonal reference line, mark a line perpendicular to it, again through the intersection of the first set of lines. Dry-fit tiles and adjust their layout as with the standard tile layout. It is best to have full tiles and half tiles in the most visible areas. Make sure your tile cutter is large enough to make diagonal trim cuts on the tile you are installing.

RUNNING BOND: Determine the final layout reference lines as in a standard tile layout (See pages 30 to 31). When balancing the tile layout, use two rows of tiles, since one row offsets the other by half a tile length. Additional grid lines are very helpful with these narrower

Floor tile types

Tiles come in a variety of sizes and shapes. Most tiles are glazed ceramic; a layer of colored glaze is baked onto the clay tile material. *Mosaic tiles* can be made of either glazed ceramic or porcelain, a harder tile material that is a uniform color throughout. *Quarry tiles* also are the same color throughout. They are softer, porous, unglazed clay tiles that are usually thicker than glazed ceramic tiles. *Natural stone tiles* are usually made from marble, slate, limestone or granite. They are much more expensive than ceramic tiles—but ceramic tiles that closely resemble natural stone are available at a fraction of their cost.

Tips for choosing tile:

- Large tiles make a room look larger; small tiles make it look smaller.
- Square tiles are the easiest to install.
- Larger tiles have fewer grout lines, requiring less installation time and maintenance.
- Small tiles, like mosaics, are usually joined together in fiber-backed sheets to make them easier to install. Unlike larger

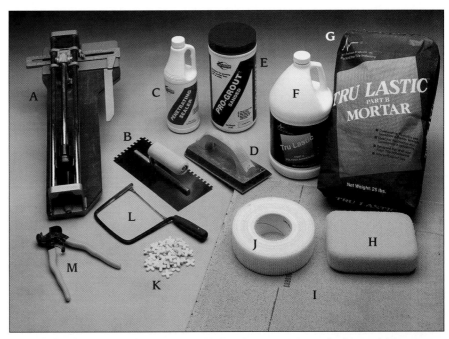

Tools and materials for installing tile include: tile cutter (A); notched trowel (B); grout sealer (C); grout float (D); grout (E); latex grout additive (F); thinset mortar (G); grout sponge (H); cementboard (I); fiberglass seam tape (J); tile spacers (K); rod saw for cutting tiles (L); and tile nippers (M).

tiles, they can be installed successfully on a floor that isn't perfectly level.
- Tiles with irregular shapes, like hexagons, take the most installation time. Some require that smaller square or round tiles be installed in the spaces between

the field tiles.
- Border, accent and base-trim tiles help create showpiece floors but require extra work.
- Glazed tiles have different finishes that affect how easily they scratch and how slippery they are.

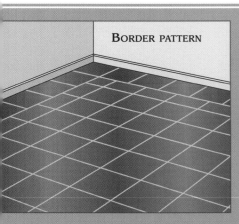

BORDER PATTERN

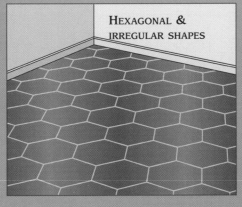

HEXAGONAL & IRREGULAR SHAPES

requiring minimal cutting of main tiles—border tiles should remain full-size. After adjusting the layout, snap perpendicular lines for the main tiles and also for the border tiles. You can combine several design elements, using border tiles between different patterns or shaped tiles. Simply follow the layout instructions from the appropriate pattern.

HEXAGONAL & IRREGULAR SHAPES: Determine the final layout reference lines as in a standard tile layout. When balancing the tile layout, dry-fit enough tiles to be certain a properly aligned pattern is tested. Additional grid lines may be very helpful for keeping irregular tile shapes aligned during installation. Make certain to allow for proper spacing between tiles. Spread mortar on the backs of tiles that overlap reference lines.

tiles. Make certain to allow for proper spacing between tiles and the offset distance when marking grid lines. Spread mortar on the backs of tiles that overlap reference lines due to the offset.

BORDER PATTERN: Mark initial reference lines as in Steps 1 through 3 of the standard floor layout. Dry-fit main floor tiles and border tiles along the reference lines, as in Step 4, to create a balanced layout

Creating layout lines for floor tile

Before you begin laying out your floor tile project, make sure the subfloor and underlayment are in suitable condition (See pages 20 to 25). Generally, cementboard (also called concrete backerboard) is the best underlayment for tile floors in wet areas like bathrooms and kitchens. Plywood is an acceptable underlayment for floor tile in other areas, provided the combined thickness of subfloor and underlayment is at least 1¼ in. Interior-grade plywood, particleboard and chipboard are not considered suitable for use as tile underlayment. A stable concrete floor is a fine surface for tile, but it must be level, and any cracks should be covered with isolation membrane (See page 23).

You can install tile over some existing floors, including tile, if they are at least 1¼ in. thick, flat, in good repair and the floorcovering is well-bonded to the subfloor. However, keep in mind the additional floor height this creates. Also, you'll need to roughen the surface of the old floorcovering if it's too glossy. Cushioned vinyl flooring must be removed or covered with an appropriate underlayment.

Once the subfloor and underlayment are properly prepared, start your tiling project by creating layout lines with a chalkline. There is no single method or approach for selecting the best layout for any room, but keep two main principles in mind as you determine the best place to start: try to arrange the tiles so the most visible areas in the room are covered with full tiles; and try to keep cuts to a minimum. Plan on a little trial and error as you dry-lay tiles to test layouts.

HOW TO CREATE TILE LAYOUT LINES

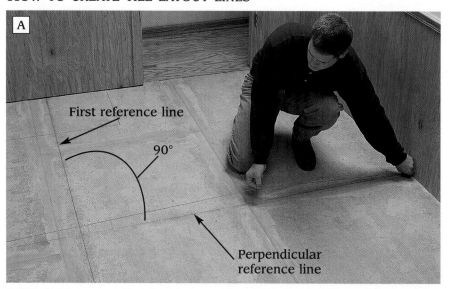

PHOTO A The process of creating a floor tile layout starts with a pair of perpendicular reference lines. Measure out from one wall at two or more points and snap the first reference line. Then, snap the second reference line perpendicular to the first. Use a carpenter's square as a guide, then check to confirm that the lines are square to one another (the 3-4-5 method works well to do this).

PHOTO B Dry-lay tiles along one reference line, working toward the wall. The seam between two tiles should align with the intersecting reference line. Measure the amount the layout needs to be adjusted so the tile next to the wall doesn't need to be cut. Shift the tiles back toward the reference line by this amount.

1 Snap a line through the central area of the floor, perpendicular to the most visible wall in the room and extending to the opposite wall **(See Photo A).** Mark another line perpendicular to the first, through the central area, extending from side wall to side wall. Make certain these two reference lines are perpendicular to ensure a good layout.

2 Dry-lay tiles along one reference line, using plastic tile spacers between tiles (See Tip, next page). Adjust the tiles in each direction along the line to create a balanced layout **(See Photo B).** If the tiles at both ends of the row will be less than half their original size, shift the row half the width of a tile in either direction. As a rule, the ends of a row should contain tiles of equal dimension. But if only one row end is visible, begin

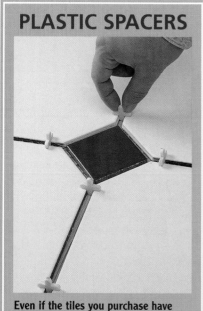
with a full tile at the visible end and conceal any cut tiles at the other end (under cabinets, behind doors or around corners). Keep in mind the position of any outside wall corners relative to tile seams when adjusting this row. Also keep in mind that it is difficult and not recommended to cut and install pieces of tile less than a third of their original size.

3 After adjusting this row, snap a new reference line, running through a tile seam at the center of the layout area, parallel to the reference line you snapped perpendicular to the first reference line **(See Photo C).** Use a different chalk color or erase the first line to prevent confusion when laying tiles. Dry-fit tiles along this new reference line, making adjustments as needed **(See Photo D).**

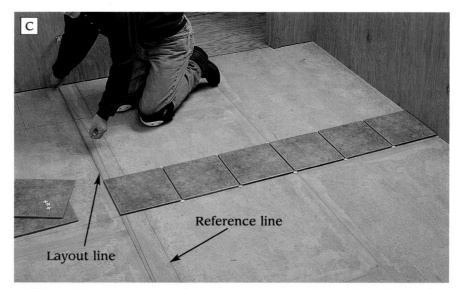

PHOTO C After adjusting the tile layout, snap a layout line parallel to the reference line. To avoid confusion, either erase the reference line or use chalk of a different color for the layout line.

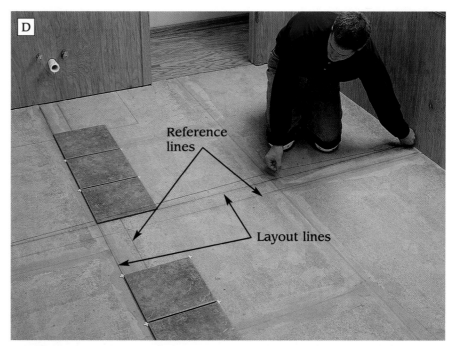

PHOTO D Snap a layout line that follows the line created by the edge of the adjusted, dry-laid tile. Make sure the new layout line is perpendicular to the first layout line and parallel to the squared reference line. Use the layout lines to divide the project into working quadrants.

4 If beginning at the intersection of the final reference lines will make it awkward to lay tile (for example, in a long, thin room) mark additional lines in a grid so you can install the tiles in sections. Make certain that grid lines run at seams between tiles and are parallel to the reference lines. If you are installing irregularly shaped tile or using a non-square layout configu-ration, make additional layout lines as needed.

TIP: If you're renting a tile cutter, consider dry-laying the entire floor and marking all the tiles that need cutting so you can cut them efficiently while the tool is in your possession (See page 35).

CUTTING TILE WITH A WET SAW

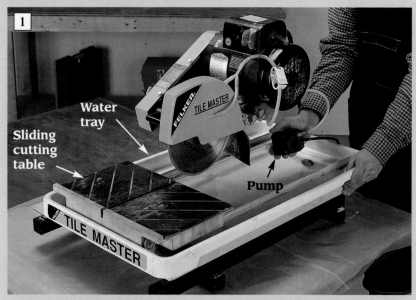

Water tray

Sliding cutting table

Pump

STEP 1: Fill the water tray with water according to the manufacturer's recommendations, then hook up the pump and hoses. Set the pump in the tray.

STEP 2: Place the tile to be cut face-up on the sliding cutting table, making sure the cutting line is aligned with the blade. Turn on the saw and feed the tile into the blade by pushing the table forward.

Wet saws for cutting tiles can be rented at most rental centers. Tell the rental agent what type of material you'll be cutting so he can fit the saw with the appropriate blade. Also make sure to get specific operating instructions.

To economize on the rental fee, premark all the tiles you'll need to cut before renting the wet saw. Be aware that many rental companies will measure the blade teeth before and after you use the saw and charge a blade wear fee in addition to the rental rate.

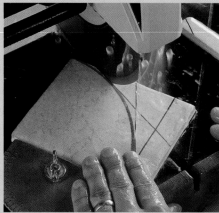

TIP: To make curved cuts with a wet saw, remove the waste with several straight cuts that are tangent to the arc of the curve. If necessary, clean up the cutting line with nippers.

Cutting floor tiles

Which method you choose to cut floor tile should depend primarily on two variables: the number and type of cuts you'll need to make, and the thickness and hardness of the tiles. If you've ever installed wall tile, the chances are good that you've used a hand-operated tile cutter like the one shown at the bottom of the next page. These inexpensive tools are especially good for making straight cuts on thinner wall tiles, but they can also handle ceramic floor tiles. If you're cutting porcelain tile or natural stone, however, you should look into another option, like a wet saw (See photos, left). Also, for cutting more than a handful of ceramic floor tiles, the hand-operated tile cutter will probably tax your patience, if not your reserves of elbow grease.

Wet saws can be rented by the day at most rental centers. For just about any floor tiling project, you'll find them to be a good investment. You can even use them to do most of the hard work when making curved cuts. Tile nippers can also be used for curved cuts, but they have the same restrictions that apply to hand-operated tile cutters.

Perhaps the best option is simply to figure out how your layout will look and have the tiles cut to fit by your tile distributor. The small fee is usually more than offset by the savings you'll realize on time and waste caused by breaking or miscutting tiles.

Working Safely

Wear eye protection whenever you cut or break ceramic or stone tile. Also, wear gloves when handling cut tile edges, which can be very sharp. Use a hand-held grinding stone or tile sander to smooth these edges when the tile will be exposed, such as at a threshold. Kneepads provide protection and comfort on hard floor surfaces.

How to Cut Curves in Tile

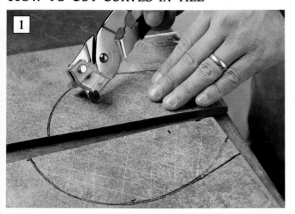

STEP 1: To make curved cuts in ceramic or stone tile, start by scoring the cutting line onto the surface of the tile with a tile scoring tool. To make the waste easier to remove, also score cutting lines in a cross-hatch pattern across the waste area.

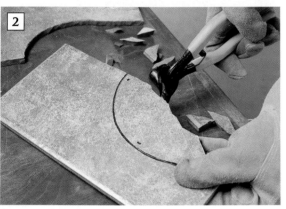

STEP 2: Snap off small pieces of the waste tile with tile nippers. You'll get best results if you break the tile along the scored cross-hatch lines. Work your way toward the curved cutting line. Avoid getting too greedy as you work—trying to remove too much waste at once can cause the tile to fracture in half. Wear gloves and eye protection when using tile nippers.

TIP: A carbide-tipped hole saw and drill can be used to make circular cutouts in tile. Be sure to secure the tile to your worksurface and place a backer board underneath the tile.

How to Use a Tile Cutter

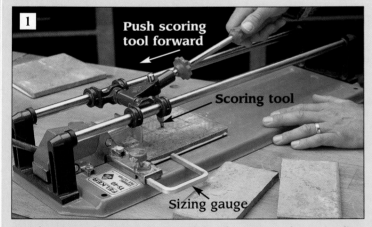

Push scoring tool forward

Scoring tool

Sizing gauge

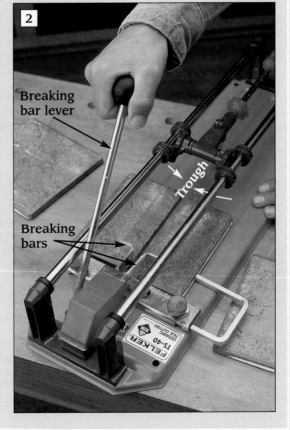

Breaking bar lever

Trough

Breaking bars

1 (Above) Set the tile on the bed of the tile cutter so the cutting line is aligned with the point of the scoring tool. Some tile cutters, like the one above, are equipped with a sizing gauge so you can set the tool to make multiple cuts that are the same width. Lighter duty cutters often cut on the pull stroke, but the rented, heavy-duty model shown here cuts on the push stroke. Press down on the lever that lowers the scoring tool and push forward, scoring the cutting line.

2 (Right) Retract the scoring tool clear of the tile, then lower the lever that controls the breaking bars. These bars exert downward pressure toward the trough in the center of the bed, causing the tile to snap along the scored line.

Choose the best trowel for the job

Use a steel trowel with the appropriately sized and shaped notches to apply the proper amount of thinset mortar or ceramic tile adhesive for the tile you install. Always check the thinset or adhesive product manufacturer's instructions for trowel recommendations. Generally, larger and more uneven tiles require thicker adhesive beds.

³⁄₈-in. V-notched trowel for mosaic sheets.

³⁄₄-in. square-notched trowel for tiles smaller than 12 × 12 in.

½-in. square-notched trowel for larger tiles and natural stone tile.

Laying floor tiles

Whether your tile is made of ceramic, porcelain or natural stone, the process for installing it is essentially the same. The primary variable is the thickness of the thinset mortar bed required for each type of tile (See *Choose the Best Trowel for the Job,* left). For larger tiling projects, you can break the job up into smaller working sections, then tile one or two sections every weekend. If you go this route, protect the new tile and the underlayment with sheeting or plywood when you're not working on it. Wait until all the tile is installed before grouting.

Before you begin actually setting tiles into the thinset mortar, prepare the project area by:
- Inspecting and repairing the subfloor, if needed (Pages 20 to 25).
- Installing a suitable floor underlayment product—for wet areas, use cementboard (Page 25). Make sure the underlayment is clean of debris before you get to work.
- Snapping perpendicular reference and layout lines based on a dry-lay of the tiles (Pages 30 to 31).

Mixing thinset mortar

Thinset mortar is mortar that's formulated to be applied in a thin bed for ceramic and stone tiles. It comes in dry mix (shown above) and premixed forms. Each 50-pound bag of dry mix will cover as much as 100 sq. ft. of floor area, depending on the size of the trowel used to apply it. For quick mixing, pour the ingredients in a 5-gallon bucket and mix with a mixing attachment chucked into an electric drill. Since dry-mix thinset has an open time of up to two hours, you can mix it in fairly large batches. To make the mortar more flexible (and less likely to crack), add acrylic fortifier to the mixture.

1 Mix thinset adhesive mortar by adding liquid a little at a time to the dry material, according to the manufacturer's directions. The proper mixture should be just stiff enough to hold "peaks," like whipped cream. Mix only as much thinset as you can use in 30 minutes or so. If the old mixture starts to stiffen before you've used it, discard it and prepare a fresh batch.

2 Beginning at the point of intersection between the layout lines, apply a layer of thinset approximately 3 × 3 ft., using the correct-sized trowel for your tile (See *Sidebar,* left). We used a ¼-in. square-notched trowel for the 12 × 12 in. ceramic tiles we chose **(See Photo A).** Make furrows in the mortar, holding the notched edge of the trowel consistently at a 45° angle to the floor. Don't cover up the layout lines—they must be visible for tile alignment. Wear rubber gloves when working with cementitious products like thinset.

When to cut tiles

There are two schools of thought on which is the better time to cut tiles: before you begin laying tile or during the installation. If you're renting a wet saw, you may want to avoid laying tile while the rental fee clock is running by marking tiles for cutting during the dry-lay process, then cutting all the tiles to fit before you start laying the tile floor. But the best way to ensure professional-looking results is to cut the tiles to fit after all the uncut tiles in each working quadrant are laid. If you choose this approach, make sure you don't apply the thinset adhesive until all the tiles for that section are cut to fit. Whether you're cutting before or during the tile-laying process, mark and make cuts using the techniques shown on pages 32 to 33 and 36 to 37.

HOW TO INSTALL FLOOR TILE

PHOTO A Begin at the intersection of the perpendicular layout lines (See pages 30 to 31) and spread thinset adhesive with the flat edge of the trowel along both reference lines in one quadrant. Don't cover up the lines—they must be visible for tile alignment. Spread only enough thinset to cover an area about 2 × 2 ft. in this quadrant of the layout. Make furrows in the mortar, holding the notched edge of the trowel consistently at a 45° angle to the floor.

PHOTO B Set the first tile in the corner of the quadrant, twisting it slightly as you press it into the thinset mortar. Gently rap the center area of the tile, using a soft-rubber mallet, to make certain it is set evenly in the mortar. **TIP:** If you install mosaic sheets, use a grout float to set a sheet after positioning it in the mortar (see inset photo), without twisting or using the mallet.

PHOTO C Place plastic tile spacers at the corners of this first tile. Tile spacers ensure consistent spacing between tiles and even alignment. Position and set the two adjacent tiles along the layout lines and against the spacers. NOTE: If you install mosaic sheets, use tile spacers equal in width to the gaps between individual tiles within the sheet.

PHOTO D Fill out the tile project area, working in smaller sections. After each section is completed, even out the tile surfaces with a mallet and padded 2 × 4. Don't get so aggressive here that you displace the mortar.

Tips & Tricks for Trimming Tile

Marking for a straight cut: To mark a tile for cutting at the end of a run where it meets the wall, lay tiles up to the last uncut tile in the row. Then, position the tile to be cut directly on top of the last uncut tile. As a spacer, set a third full tile on top of the tile to be cut, but position it so the end butts against the wall (leave a gap of 1/4 in. or so at the wall). Mark a line along the edge where the top tile overlaps the trimming tile. The visible portion of the tile to be cut is installed.

Installing cut tiles: It is often difficult to apply an even layer of thinset adhesive to the floor in tight areas where you'll be installing cut tiles. In such cases, you'll get better results by "buttering" the back of the tile with the trowel, then setting the tile piece in position.

Cutting around obstructions: Measure the location of the obstruction (a closet flange for a toilet is shown here) relative to adjacent tiles, then mark reference points for the cutout on the tile to be cut. Allow for the spaces between tiles. Outline the cutout based on the markings then cut the tile (See pages 32 to 33).

Cabinet areas: You can usually conserve time and tiles by leaving out floor tiles that will be concealed by cabinetry. In the photo above, the tiles are stopped about 1 in. inside the planned edges of the vanity cabinet location.

Cutting tiles for corners: Set the tile to be cut directly on top of the full tile nearest the corner, then set a spacer tile on top of the full tile and butt it up against the wall in one direction, as shown in the left photo at the top of this page. Mark a cutting line on the tile to be cut (PHOTO 1). Then re-position the spacer tile so it butts against the other wall forming the corner. Mark the tile to be cut (PHOTO 2). The corner of the tile opposite the wall corner will fit the corner opening perfectly.

Marking for a straight cut

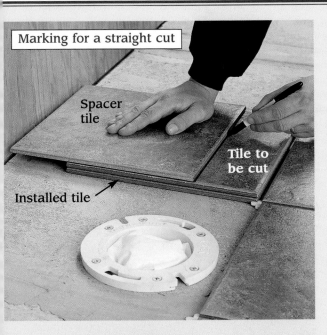

Spacer tile

Tile to be cut

Installed tile

Installing cut tiles

Cutting around obstructions

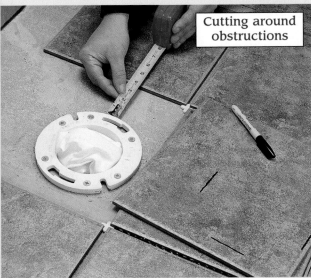

Cabinet areas

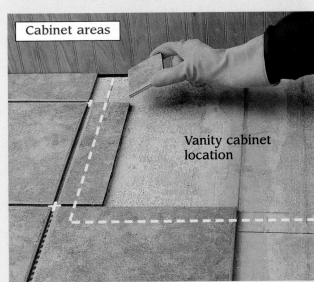

Vanity cabinet location

HOW TO CUT TILES FOR CORNERS

1

Spacer tile

Tile to be cut

2

Spacer tile

Tile to be cut

PHOTO E Remove the plastic spacers before the thinset mortar has dried completely (they're much harder to get out after the mortar sets). While some installers maintain that the spacers may be left in place without weakening the grout lines, we've had better luck and cleaner results with them removed.

PHOTO F The primary access spot to the room being tiled should be the last section you tile. Once the tiles are installed, avoid walking on them for at least eight hours and preferably a full day. Wait a minimum of 24 hours before applying grout.

3 Set the first tile in the corner of the quadrant, twisting it slightly as you press it into the thinset **(See Photo B).** Very gently, rap the center area of the tile, using a soft-rubber mallet, to make certain it is set evenly in the mortar. If you are installing mosaic sheets, use a grout float to set each sheet after positioning it in the mortar **(See inset, Photo B).**

4 Place plastic tile spacers at the corners of this first tile. We used ¼-in. spacers, since that is the recommended gap thickness for 12 × 12-in. tiles. Install tiles along one leg of the layout quadrant, butting the new tiles up against the spacers. Insert spacers and set tiles along the other leg of the quadrant, up to the end of the thinset-covered work area **(See Photo C).** Tile spacers ensure consistent spacing between tiles and even alignment. Clean any mortar from the tile surface as soon as possible, using a damp rag.

5 Fill out the field area of the working quadrant section. Always work from the layout lines toward the open area of the quadrant to ensure accurate tile alignment. Lay a straight, 3- to 4-ft.-long piece of padded 2 × 4 across the tiles and rap along the top with a rubber mallet to ensure that adjacent tiles are level **(See Photo D).**

6 After an area of tile is set in mortar, remove the plastic spacers before the mortar dries (prying out spacers from hardened mortar may damage tile edges). Check all the seams and remove excess mortar (grout must be able to fully penetrate the seam) using a putty knife or small trowel **(See Photo E).** Also clean any mortar off of tile surfaces before it hardens. Finish each quadrant before beginning the next one.

7 Fill out the rest of the quadrant, applying the adhesive and laying tile in small sections **(See Photo F).** Work in a pattern so you don't have

Tips for doorways & thresholds

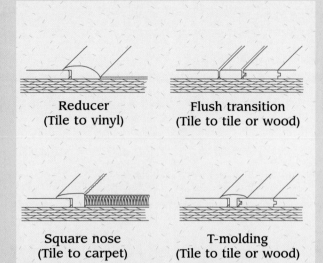

Reducer
(Tile to vinyl)

Flush transition
(Tile to tile or wood)

Square nose
(Tile to carpet)

T-molding
(Tile to tile or wood)

It usually is easier to cut off the bottom of jamb molding than it is to mark and cut the tile to fit around it. Use a jamb saw, which is designed to cut while resting on a flat surface. Determine the height of a tile set in thinset mortar (usually the thickness of the tile plus 1/8 in.). Add a spacer to a piece of tile so their combined thickness is about 1/16 in. more than this height, and place them next to the jamb molding (protect the tile surface by placing the spacer piece on top of the tile). Rest the jamb saw on the spacer and cut the jamb molding.

Transition strips are needed whenever you move from one floor covering material to another. This is especially true of tile floor, since they're frequently higher than other floor coverings in the home. If the tile floor and the adjoining surface are at the same height, choose a flat tile or solid-surface transition strip that is set directly into thinset. If one floor surface is higher than the other, you may be able to find a tile transition strip that's beveled to create a small ramp between the surfaces, but more likely you'll need to look for a beveled wood transition strip.

G

PHOTO G Install the transition piece you've selected in the doorway. The one being installed here is made from solid-surfacing material, and is set directly into a bed of thinset mortar. In situations where the two floorcoverings are at the same height, a flat transition piece should be used. But if one surface is higher than the other, as is often the case with floors that are remodeled with tile, then you'll need a transition piece that is angled or stepped down to create a mini step from the higher surface to the lower surface (See Illustrations, above). Between the transition and the tile, make sure to maintain a gap the same thickness as the gaps between tiles (**inset photo**).

PHOTO H Use a grout float to apply the grout mixture to the floor. Hold the float at an angle of around 35°, working the grout material into the seams between tiles.

PHOTO I Once the seams are full of grout, use the edge of the grout float to scrape excess grout from the tile surfaces. Drag diagonally across the tiles to remove excess grout.

Mixing Grout

For almost all floor tile installations, use sanded grout to fill the seams between tiles. Typically it is sold as a dry mix that's blended with water to the proper consistency, then pressed into the seams with a grout float. When dried, it is not as hard and dense as the thinset mortar used to create the tile bed. This allows for some slight expansion and movement of the floorcovering without cracking of the tiles. Most grout manufacturers today have a polymerized additive blended in at the plant so no latex or acrylic additives are required (or even advisable).

Grout mix comes in a variety of colors to blend in to or contrast with your tile.

Mix grout in relatively small batches using only cool, clean water. When properly blended, the grout mixture should have a stiff, creamy consistency.

PHOTO J Dampen a clean sponge with cold water, wring it out and use it to wipe the remaining grout residue from the tile surfaces. Work diagonally across the grout lines to help prevent disturbing them. Rotate the sponge after each pass, and rinse it clean often.

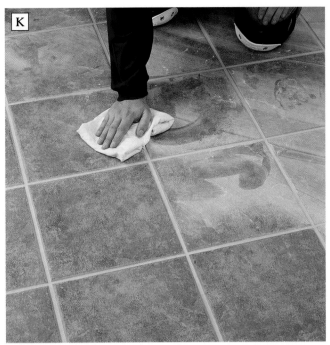

PHOTO K After the grout has cured for two or three hours, polish the tiles with a soft cloth to remove any dried grout residue. Take care not to dislodge the grout from the seams. TIP: Stubborn grout stains on open-pore tiles can be removed with exterior deck-washing products or, in more extreme cases, highly diluted muriatic acid.

to kneel on tiles that have been laid before the thinset has set up (usually at least 8 hours). If you must work on tile before the thinset is completely dry, kneel on a piece of ¾ in. plywood that is 2 × 2 ft. or larger to distribute your weight. As you work, you may find that your speed increases and you're able to increase the size of the working sections as a result. When you reach the walls or encounter obstructions, you'll generally need to trim the tiles to fit. See the tips and tricks shown on pages 36 to 37 for information on how to mark and cut tiles to fit specific spots. Also, see pages 32 to 33 for information on how to cut floor tiles.

8 You'll likely need to trim off the bottoms of the door jambs for the threshold and the tiles in the doorway area to fit correctly. Cut and install a threshold in the doorway, keeping the same spacing between it and the adjacent tiles as there is between the rest of the tiles **(See Photo G and *Tips for doorways & thresholds*, page 39).** If you're installing a ceramic, stone or solid-surface material threshold, set it in thinset so its top is flush with the surface of the adjacent tiles. The surface of a wood threshold should also be flush with the tiles. Let the mortar on the entire floor cure for at least 24 hours.

9 Mix enough floor grout for roughly a 20-square-foot area, adding latex grout additive in small

amounts until the mixture reaches a 'toothpaste' consistency **(See *Mixing Grout*, previous page)** and be sure to follow the grout manufacturer's directions).

10 Pour the grout mixture onto the tile, beginning in a corner. Use a grout float to spread and force the grout into the spaces between tiles **(See Photo H).** Grout isn't necessary in spaces that will be covered by base-trim tiles or other molding. Hold the float at a 35° angle to the floor and move it in a figure-eight pattern until the spaces are completely filled in the small area you are working. Cover the surface of a wood threshold with masking tape before grouting to prevent damage.

11 Remove as much excess grout as possible by holding the float almost perpendicular to the tile and scraping it diagonally across the seams **(See Photo I).** Spread and remove excess grout until about 20 square feet of floor has been grouted.

12 Wipe a damp sponge diagonally across the seams and tile surface to remove remaining excess grout **(See Photo J).** Hold the sponge flat and don't press too hard or wipe too much, which can pull grout from the seams. Rinse the sponge frequently in cold water, and change the water often.

13 Continue spreading and removing excess grout on the rest of the floor. Let the grout dry for about three hours (check manufacturer's directions for exact drying times), then use a soft cloth to polish the tiles, removing any remaining grout film **(See Photo K).** Let the grout cure completely.

14 Apply grout sealer to the grouted seams, using a sponge brush **(See Photo L).** Keep sealer off of tile surfaces and remove any excess immediately. Let sealer dry at least 8 hours (check manufacturer's directions). On porous or unglazed tiles, you may want to apply tile sealer to the surfaces of the installed tiles **(See *Sealing Quarry Tile*, below).**

PHOTO L The grout lines should be sealed periodically with grout sealer to protect the soft grout from moisture penetration by mildew and mold. Reseal every few months if the floor receives heavy traffic and is cleaned frequently, otherwise, every 6 to 8 months is adequate. If the grout is clean and stable, apply new sealer with a foam brush, wiping excess from the tile surface before it dries.

Sealing Quarry Tile

The softer, porous material and natural color of quarry tile make it an excellent interior floor surface. But because of these features, it can also be stained easily. To help prevent staining, apply a porous tile sealer to the entire floor before grouting. Then apply sealer to the grout lines after you've grouted to seal the seams.

Spread the sealer using either a paint brush or a paint roller with a thin-nap sleeve and an extension handle. If you choose to let the quarry tile "weather" naturally, carefully seal the grout with grout sealer—the tile will turn a darker color wherever grout sealer touches it.

Installing base tiles

Base tiles are installed at the bottom of a wall to transition between a tile floor and the wall surfaces. They are formed with coves on the bottoms so they can better conceal gaps between the floor tiles and the walls, and to help shed water. Base tiles can be purchased in the same color and styles as most ceramic or porcelain floor tiles. In some cases, however, preformed base tiles will not be available. This is particularly true of stone tiles, which, oddly enough, don't occur in nature with regular cove lips. In such cases, it is common practice to cut pieces of floor tile into strips, usually about 3 in. wide, and bond them to the wall. Contrasting ceramic quarter round trim tiles can be applied over the top edge of the strips to soften their appearance and edge. Or, you may want to to use near-matching or contrasting base tiles for the whole base area. Wood or vinyl cove base molding is another option.

Base tiles generally are shorter than the full width of the floor tiles, so it is not reasonable to expect your grout lines to line up between the floor and the wall. When purchasing base tiles, plan your layout ahead of time: you'll need a double-bullnose corner tile for each corner in the room.

As with floor tile, a dry-run will help you create a base tile layout that minimizes cutting and positions any cut tiles in low-visibility spots (for example, behind a toilet). Wherever possible, avoid cutting the premitered corner tiles.

1 Once you've established a layout plan, begin the installation by installing both corner tiles at an outside corner—more than any others, these are the tiles you want to avoid cutting. Spread ceramic wall-tile adhesive on the backs of the tiles, using a notched trowel specified by the adhesive manufacturer—a ³⁄₁₆ in. V-notched trowel is

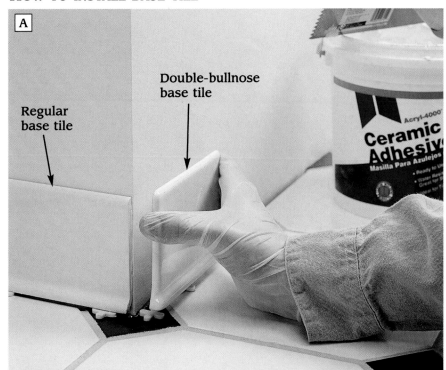

PHOTO A Begin laying base tile at an outside corner. Install a full tile so the edge is flush with the corner, then overlap it with a double-bullnose tile. Set each tile on plastic spacers and bond them to the wall with ceramic wall tile adhesive applied with a notched trowel.

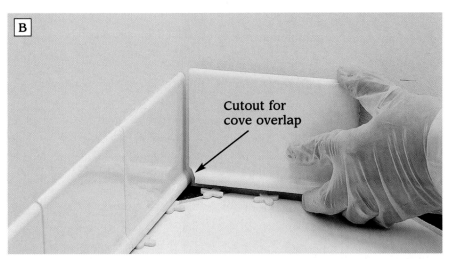

PHOTO B The overlapping corner of the cove needs to be trimmed to fit over the adjoining tile at inside corners. The easiest way to make this cut is with a rod saw. Wherever possible, use full tiles at inside corners as well as outside corners.

typical (See page 34). Insert plastic spacers beneath the tiles, and also between tiles as you work your way along the wall. Press the tiles onto the wall with a slight twisting motion and hold them in place momentarily to make sure they stick. At outside corners, one tile should be flush with the edge of

the corner. Use a double-bullnose tile to cover the edge of this tile from the other side of the corner **(See Photo A).** Leave a slight gap for grout at corner joints.

2 At inside corners, mark and cut one tile to fit around the curved profile of the other **(See Photo B).**

How to install base tile (continued)

PHOTO C Remove the spacers and apply clear silicone caulk in the expansion gap between the base-trim tiles and the floor. Clear caulk allows the color of tile and colored grout to show through, disguising the seam. You can use white kitchen/bathroom caulk if the grout is white.

Use a rod saw (See page 29) or a jig saw and tungsten-carbide blade to cut the cove profile.

3 Continue installing base-trim tiles, cutting tiles where necessary **(See *Cutting Base Tiles*, below).**

4 After installing all the base-trim tiles, remove the plastic spacers and let the adhesive dry for at least 8 hours (check manufacturer's directions). Grout and seal the vertical seams (See page 42) and caulk the gap between floor tiles and base tiles **(See Photo C).** Use painter's masking tape to protect finished wall surfaces from grout.

CUTTING BASE TILES

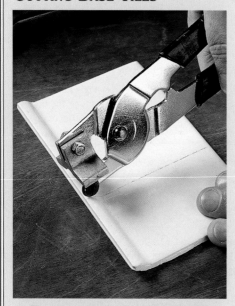

1 The cove portion on base tiles presents a bit of a challenge for cutting. First, draw a cutting line on the tile. Holding the tile securely (or better yet, clamping it carefully to the worksurface), score the cove portion of the cut with a tile scoring tool. Make several light to medium passes with the tool—heavy pressure can break the tile.

2 Set the base tile to be cut in the bed of your tile cutter so the scored line on the cove aligns with the cutting mechanism on the tile cutter. Score the tile up to the base of the cove using the cutting tool on the tile cutter. Then, snap the tile along the cutting line as you would break a square field tile (See page 33).

Maintenance & repair

Routine maintenance: In addition to regular cleaning of the tiled floor, the grout lines should be sealed periodically with grout sealer to prevent moisture penetration and mold/mildew accumulation. Do this every few months if the floor receives heavy traffic and is cleaned frequently, otherwise, every 6 to 8 months should suffice. If the grout is clean and stable, apply new sealer with a foam brush, wiping excess from the tile surface before it dries.

Regrouting: Grout is considerably less long-lasting than the tile itself, and from time to time you'll need to scrape out the old grout and replace it with fresh material (you'll be amazed at the difference this makes in the appearance of the floor). To regrout, remove loose or moldy grout with a grout saw **(See Photo A, right).** Scrub the grout lines clean then reapply grout the same way you applied it originally (See pages 40 to 42). Generally, it's best to clean and regrout the entire floor at the same time.

Replacing damaged tiles: Use a grout saw to remove grout around the damaged tile **(See Photo A)** or around a section of damaged tiles. Break the damaged tile into small pieces, using a hammer and nailset or small mason's chisel **(See Photo B).** Always wear eye protection when breaking tile as pieces may fly several feet. Use a putty knife or mason's chisel to scrape away tile pieces and old mortar and grout. Get the tile underlayment surface as clean and smooth as possible. Remove all debris with a vacuum cleaner.

Spread thinset mortar on the back of the tile (or on the floor area if replacing a section of tile). It's better to go a little heavy on the thinset: it's easier to press the tile down until it's level with the others, then clean up any displaced thinset, than it is to remove the tile and add more thinset to

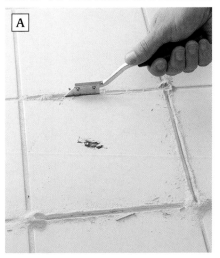

PHOTO A Use a grout saw to remove grout around the damaged tile or tiles.

PHOTO B Break the damaged tile into small pieces and scrape the floor smooth.

PHOTO C Apply thinset mortar to the back of the tile (or to the underlayment if replacing multiple tiles) and position the tile. Press down on the tile until it's level with the surrounding tiles. Wipe up any excess thinset that squeezes out and, if necessary, remove thinset from the gaps with the grout saw to create room for the new grout.

PHOTO D Mix and apply new grout around the tile or tiles. Generally, fresh grout will be lighter in color than old grout, so you may want to choose grout mix that's tinted a shade darker then the original grout used.

raise the tile. Set the tile or tiles in position **(See Photo C).** The surface of the new tile should be flush with the adjacent tiles. Let the mortar dry according to the manufacturer's directions.

Mix a small amount of matching grout and grout the seams around the new tile or tiles **(See Photo D).**

If replacing one small tile or a small area of damaged grout, you can use your fingers to force grout into the seams, then remove the excess with a damp sponge. Apply grout sealer after the grout has cured. See pages 36 to 42 for more information on installing floor tiles and applying grout.

Wood Floors

A wood floor offers a vibrant surface, rich with texture and natural color. It gives your home a warm, inviting atmosphere. Wood flooring well serves most decorating styles and often is the showpiece of a room, particularly when given special decorative treatment. Wood also is a durable and forgiving surface; most minor damage is relatively easy to repair.

The most common wood floors are still made from ¾ in. thick solid wood hardwood floorboards. But in recent years more homeowners have been installing engineered wood floor products because they are eas-

ier to work with and they're often cheaper. Another economical option to solid hardwood floors is to sand and refinish an exsiting floor. In some cases, a few simple repairs may be all you need to revive a floor. These options all are covered in the following chapter.

After you've invested time and money in a wood floor, develop a maintenance schedule to protect your investment. Clean it at least once a week with a vacuum or dust mop—dust and other debris can scratch and dull a finish quickly. Wipe up spills immediately. A damp mop is good for most general cleanups. Follow manufacturer's directions for other cleaning needs. Protect entryways with doormats or throw rugs. Place fabric-faced glides on all furniture legs.

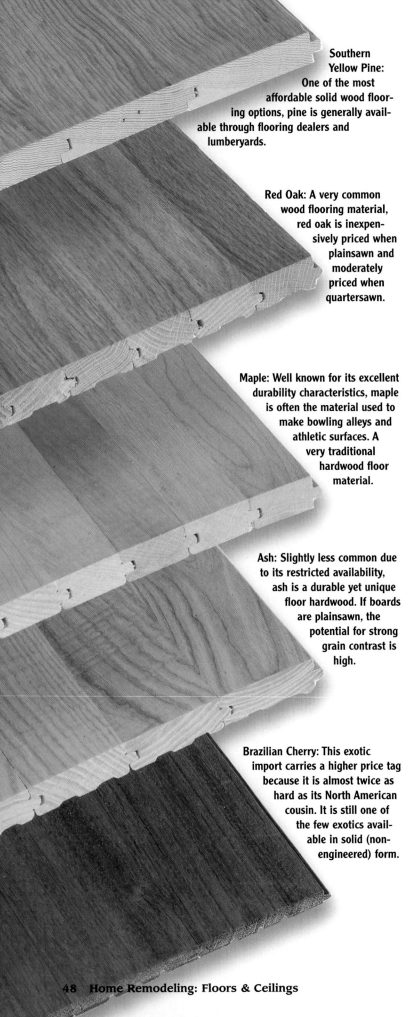

Southern Yellow Pine: One of the most affordable solid wood flooring options, pine is generally available through flooring dealers and lumberyards.

Red Oak: A very common wood flooring material, red oak is inexpensively priced when plainsawn and moderately priced when quartersawn.

Maple: Well known for its excellent durability characteristics, maple is often the material used to make bowling alleys and athletic surfaces. A very traditional hardwood floor material.

Ash: Slightly less common due to its restricted availability, ash is a durable yet unique floor hardwood. If boards are plainsawn, the potential for strong grain contrast is high.

Brazilian Cherry: This exotic import carries a higher price tag because it is almost twice as hard as its North American cousin. It is still one of the few exotics available in solid (non-engineered) form.

Choosing wood flooring

There are two basic types of wood flooring boards available: solid wood (left photos) and engineered wood (next page). Both types of boards are available in either strips or planks—less than 3 in. wide is considered strip flooring, wider boards are labeled "planks."

Solid wood flooring: Solid wood flooring is made from lumber (usually ¾ in. thick) of varying species, the most common being oak, maple, cherry, ash and pine. Solid wood flooring will last for the lifetime of a house, especially since it can be refinished several times. It also offers the richest color and greatest variety of grain patterns. This flooring comes in several grades, from select and clear (premium, knot free boards that are the most expensive) to common and #2 (less expensive but containing knots and other blemishes).

Solid wood boards must be nailed down. When installing solid wood as a remodeling project, the thickness of the boards will require trimming of doors and casings and transitions between flooring levels in bordering rooms.

Solid wood flooring is susceptible to warping, so boards must be stored in a dry, well-ventilated area. The boards should be stacked in the installation area for 2 to 3 days to acclimate prior to beginning the project. If the boards are delivered bundled, unbind them and loosely stack them so they can "breathe." This susceptibility to moisture makes solid wood a poor choice for damp areas, such as bathrooms and basements. Some manufacturers provide prefinished solid wood flooring, though only in a small choice of species and colors. While care must be taken not to scratch the surface during installation, this can speed up a project considerably.

Engineered flooring: Engineered wood flooring is essentially plywood or particleboard, with the top veneer layer made from hardwood of a wide variety of species and colors. Another type of engineered flooring, called *laminate flooring,* has a synthetic veneer bonded to the plywood or particleboard backing. This synthetic surface is made to resemble many materials, including varieties of stone as well as wood.

While the cost of engineered flooring can be as expensive, if not more expensive, than that of lower-cost solid wood boards, its ease of installation and factory-applied finish make installing it a very manageable home improvement project. Since it is basically plywood, it is more dimensionally stable, allowing installation anywhere, including basements and bathrooms. The hardwood surface veneer on quality engineered flooring is at least 1/8 in. thick, allowing for one refinishing, but this should be done by a professional. Engineered flooring is significantly thinner than solid wood flooring (generally 3/8 to 1/2 in. thick) making it a good choice when floor height is an issue. Thicker engineered boards are nailed down, and some can be either glued down to the subfloor or installed as a floating floor over a foam pad (wood glue is applied only to the tongue-and-grooved board edges). Some newer products are manufactured with a peel-off, self-adhesive backing, and others have a modified tongue-and-groove edge joining system that allows them to simply be snapped together. Check with the flooring dealer or manufacturer concerning requirements for specific flooring products.

Laminate flooring is usually the thinnest engineered wood flooring type and is most frequently installed as a floating floor over a foam pad. This makes it an excellent surface over concrete (though a vapor barrier is necessary underneath the pad). Its durable acrylic protective topcoat also makes it a good choice for kitchens and other high-traffic areas.

Manufacturers of engineered flooring usually offer flooring with either a flat or eased edge treatment on the boards. An eased edge (with either a small bevel or roundover) can help hide any unevenness between boards, but dirt will collect in the tiny groove it creates.

Buying wood flooring: Once you've made a flooring choice, take your room measurements to the flooring dealer. Determining the amount of flooring needed depends on the width of the boards, available board lengths and other factors that the dealer will be able to calculate for you. This is particularly true if your installation includes a border or other decorative treatment.

Engineered wood flooring with a real wood veneer layer (red oak is shown here) offers the natural beauty of wood combined with economy and ease of installation. It can be installed as a floating floor system or glued to the subfloor.

Similar to the wood-veneer flooring shown above it, this engineered wood product has a peel-and-stick adhesive backing for an extremely clean installation process.

Wood-veneer pattern plastic laminate: For an exotic look at an affordable price, wood veneer laminate is an excellent choice. In addition to variety, laminate flooring provides a durable surface highly resistant to scratches, indentations, burns and moisture. Impervious to dust and dirt, it allows easy cleanup in high-traffic areas like kitchens and dining rooms.

Non-wood pattern laminate: Most laminate flooring manufacturers also offer several non-wood patterned faces in their product lines. Typical options include checkerboard layouts and stone re-creations. As only the look is different, these designs maintain the same dependability as more traditional laminate products.

Solid wood flooring offers the ultimate in richness and sturdiness under foot. Most solid wood flooring products are ¾ in. thick with tongue-and-grooved edges for tight joints. Widths range from around 1 in. to 4 in. for most stock products, and lengths generally are random.

Solid wood flooring

Before the advent of manufactured flooring systems, nearly all wooden flooring was cut from raw lumber then machined with tongue-and-groove edges that allowed for a tight-fitting surface. Mostly due to the higher cost and more challenging installation procedures, many homeowners today are opting for floating floor systems and other, similar products. But despite the great advances in the look and installation processes achieved by the makers of flooring systems in recent years, even the best manufactured wood flooring systems cannot quite replicate the "feel" of a solid wood floor—the solidness underfoot, the depth and texture of the wood surface, even the sound the

floor makes when it is walked upon. If you appreciate the appeal of any of these qualities, or if you are simply a traditionalist when it comes to wood, you'll be glad you took the time to install a solid wood floor in your home.

Solid wood floors can be installed in any room in your house, but because the seams normally will separate slightly over time and the wood itself is not naturally moisture resistant, you may want to choose a better-suited product, such as vinyl or ceramic tile, for rooms that receive ongoing exposure to moisture (primarily bathrooms and kitchens). If you're installing a solid wood, tongue-and-groove floor of any significant size, rent a flooring nailer for the installation (See page 54). Make sure your subfloor is level and in good condition (See pages 20 to 25).

Common solid wood flooring types: by species (photos on pages 48 to 49)

WOOD	WIDTHS	STRENGTHS	WEAKNESSES	COST
Red Oak	1½, 2¼ in. (also parquet)	Stiff and dense, good wear and shock resistance, widely available in several types and styles	Large pores can produce strong stain contrasts when finishing.	Inexpensive
White Oak	1½, 2¼ in., (also parquet)	Highly durable, well-protected against insects and rot due to high tannic concentration	Tannins can react with certain finishes turning the wood green or brown	Moderate
Maple	1½, 2¼ in. (also parquet)	Extremely dense and strong, highly resistant to the most abrasive wear	High durability characteristics make it difficult to machine, light color can easily expose sanding marks	Moderate
Ash	1½, 2¼ in.	Hard but elastic make-up remains smooth under friction	Frequent grain variations can cause sporadic patterning	Moderate
Brazilian Cherry (Exotic)	1½, 2¼ in. (also parquet)	Extremely strong and durable, sands well, finishes to warm russet hue	High density makes it difficult to machine, darkens upon exposure to sunlight	Expensive
Pine (Southern Yellow)	3, 5 in.	Ease in finishing allows for a durable topcoat to help compensate for lack of hardness	Softness makes it vulnerable to scuffs dents and abrasions	Inexpensive

*Source: National Wood Flooring Association

Flooring materials

In addition to the flooring boards themselves, you'll need a few other materials for wood flooring projects. Purchase them from building centers or flooring stores.

• An underlayment layer protects the floorboards by absorbing shock. It also reduces squeaking and reverberation that can cause the flooring nails to loosen prematurely. Traditionally, 15-pound, asphalt-impregnated building paper (tar paper) has been used for the underlayment layer, but a newer, resin-based underlayment paper provides the same protection without the mess and smell of building paper (See photo, right).

• A reducing strip or threshold covers the transition from wood flooring to other flooring materials (See page 39).

• Wood putty, either stainable or tinted to match floor color, fills nail holes and minor damage in flooring.

• Nails are used to attach solid wood floors to the subfloor. Near walls you'll need to hand-nail using 8d finish nails or, for a little extra holding power, spiral or ring shank nails. Nail coils for flooring nailers are available wherever the tools are rented.

UNDERLAYMENT OPTIONS

15-pound, asphalt-impregnated building paper

Resin-based underlayment paper

• Polyurethane varnish, either oil- or water-based, is the standard topcoating product these days for solid wood floors. Products specially formulated for floors (usually indicated on the label) typically have a harder, glossier surface. Some solid wood flooring is available prefinished, but these are best for new-home installations.

Solid wood flooring

Installing tongue-and-groove solid wood flooring correctly is mostly a matter of patience. The relatively narrow width of the floorboards means there will be plenty of seams and plenty of nailing involved. But with the right tools (namely, a power flooring nailer) the job is not too overwhelming. And if the subfloor is reasonably level and the floorboards of good, consistent quality, you should have a relatively small amount of sanding to do once the floorboards are installed.

The trickiest part of a solid-wood flooring installation project comes near the walls, where it is impossible to reach the board edges with a power nailer. Here, you'll need to face-nail the first board (then fill the nail holes with putty). The edges of the first few rows of boards need to be hand-nailed until you're far enough away from the wall to maneuver the power nailer into position.

Before you begin, make certain the subfloor is stable and level (See pages 20 to 25 for more information on subfloors).

1 Choose a wall running perpendicular to the floor joists as the starting wall for the installation. Mark joist positions on this wall and on the opposite wall, using the nailing pattern of the subfloor as a guide (make the marks near the bottom of the wall, where they will be covered by trim). Beginning at the wall opposite the starting wall, staple strips of resin paper underlayment (See page 51) or 15-pound building paper parallel to the wall, overlapping strips by 3 in.

2 Snap chalklines onto the underlayment between the reference marks on the walls to indicate the positions of the floor joists **(See Photo A).**

3 Mark the midpoints of the walls that run parallel to the floor

HOW TO INSTALL SOLID WOOD FLOORING

PHOTO A Install the underlayment layer (we used special resin paper—See page 51), then carefully lay out and mark reference lines along the centerlines of the floor joists. Mark joist locations on the walls before you lay the underlayment.

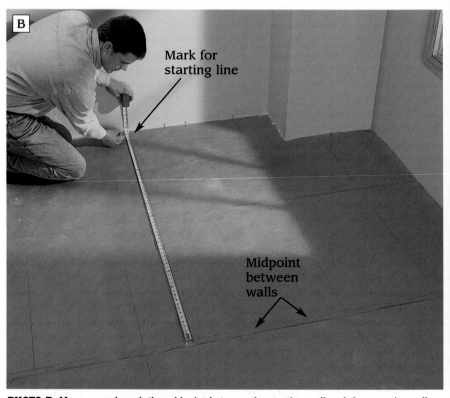

PHOTO B Measure and mark the midpoint between the starting wall and the opposite wall. Mark the midpoint at several locations, then snap a chalkline connecting the marks. Then, measure from the midpoint line toward the starting wall and mark for a starting line that is parallel to the midpoint line, about ½ in. from the wall.

PHOTO C After face-nailing the floorboards closest to the starting wall, drill pilot holes through the top of the tongue and down at a 45° angle into the floor. Drive 8d finish nails or flooring nails through the tongues and set the heads with a nailset.

PHOTO D Plan your layout as you go. The main objective is to make sure the end seams where boards butt together are offset by at least 6 in. in adjoining rows. Lay out enough boards for 7 or 8 rows at a time to create an arrangement that is adequately offset and makes efficient use of the floorboards.

joists, then snap a chalkline between the points to establish the center of the room. Measure and mark equal distances from this centerline to within ½ in. of the starting wall and snap a chalkline between the marks **(See Photo B)**. Double-check to make sure the chalkline is the same distance from the center reference line at all points. This line is used to align the first row of floorboards, ensuring that the boards in the center of the room look square to the walls, even if the room is not square. Base trim will cover the ½-in. gap and any minor variations in the gap width.

4 Align the grooved edge of a long flooring board with the starting line. Drill pilot holes for 8d finish or flooring nails and face nail this board into the subfloor 1 in. from each end, at each joist and halfway between the joists. The nails should be 1 in. in from the grooved edge and angled into the subfloor for better holding power. Set the nailheads into the counter-sink holes with a nailset. Then, drill pilot holes and drive nails at a 45° angle just above the top edge of the tongue. This is called "blind nailing" since the upper lip of the adjacent board's groove edge will cover the nailheads. Blind-nail at every joist, halfway between joists and within 2 in. of the board ends, then set the naiheads **(See Photo C)**. If installing wide plank flooring, face-nailing and blind nailing should be done every 4 to 6 in. between joists.

5 Position and nail the rest of the first course of boards, interlocking the ends by fitting the tongue-and-groove joints together **(See Photo D)**. Cut the last board to length, if necessary, using a power miter saw. Then, loosely arrange the next seven or eight rows of boards, staggering end seams in adjoining rows by at least 6 in. (preferably more). Leave a ½-in. expansion gap at all walls.

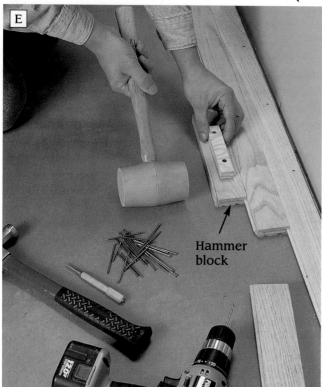

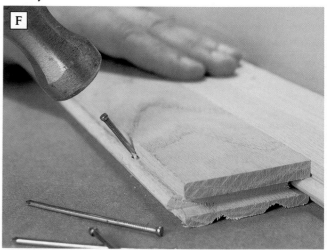

PHOTO F Drive nails through slanting pilot holes in the tops of the tongues. To avoid damaging the board, stop hammering well before the nailhead reaches the wood surface and finish driving the nails using a nailset. Use care here: one misdirected hammer blow can cause considerable damage to the edge and surface of a floorboard.

PHOTO E Make a hammer block from a piece of scrap flooring by cutting off the tongue to provide an even surface that can be driven with a mallet. Attach a small wood scrap to the top of the block for use as a handle. Start nailing at one end of the board and work toward the other end, using the hammer block to force the tongue-and-groove joint together tightly as needed.

6 Position the first second-row board with its grooved edge over the tongue of the first-row board. Use a hammer block (a 1-ft.-long scrap piece of flooring with the tongue trimmed off) and rubber mallet to drive the board tight against the first-row board **(See Photo E).** Drill pilot holes and blind-nail at every joist, halfway between the joists and within 2 in. of the board ends **(See Photo F).** If the board is slightly bowed, position and blind-nail one end before forcing the board into position. Do not use boards that are seriously bowed. Either cut them into shorter lengths, which reduces the amount of bowing in each piece, or reject them.

7 Continue positioning and blind nailing the remaining second row and the third row. Beginning with the fourth row, you should be able to use the power nailer, which drives and sets a nail in one quick stroke **(See Photo G).** Follow the manufacturer's instructions for operating the nailer. Use a nailset to set any nailheads that don't penetrate completely. If you are installing plank flooring, the power nailer usually can be used on the second course. NOTE: When nailing engineered boards that are thinner than solid wood

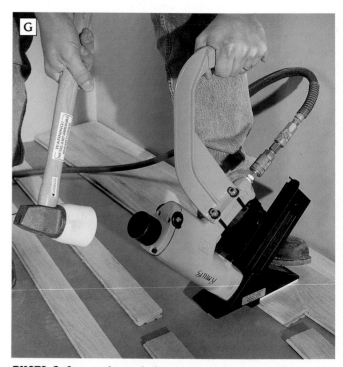

PHOTO G Once you've worked your way out from the wall a few rows, you should be able to maneuver a power flooring nailer into position. Whether it's compressor driven, like the one above, or relies on the force of the hammer blow to drive nails, flooring nailers will speed up your work tremendously, help you align the boards for tighter joints and minimize the risk of damaging floorboards.

flooring, the power nailer may require a shim so it drives nails at the proper location. Check with the rental center for the requirements of the nailer you are renting.

Working around obstructions

Rectangular openings:

It is easier to make cuts for rectangular openings, such as floor vents, after the flooring is installed than during the installation. Measure from the wall or a nearby permanent obstruction to mark a spot for a ½-in. access hole over the floor opening before installing the floorboards (stuff rags into the opening to keep debris out of air ducts). After the floorboards are installed, drill the hole, then use a jig saw to make the cutout.

Round openings and obstructions:

Use a hole saw to cut openings for pipes or other round obstructions. The hole should be about ¼ in. larger than the pipe diameter. If the pipe falls within one board, remove the pipe after measuring and marking its location if at all possible. Otherwise you will need to cut from the hole to one edge, using a jig saw, and then glue this cutout piece in place. Caulk around the obstruction after the floor finish is applied.

Outside corners:

When you reach an outside corner, make a cutting template out of cardboard to mark the floorboard that aligns with the corner for an accurate cut. Remember to allow for the ½-in. expansion gap. Use a jig saw to make the cut. To minimize tearout from the jig saw blade, cut the board with the underside facing up—be sure to orient the template correctly when you tape it to the floorboard you're cutting (it's very easy to get it backwards when you're flipping the board over for cutting).

PHOTO H Continue working toward the opposite wall of the room. Before installing each course, check to make sure that all nail heads are recessed so they don't interfere with the tongue and grove joints. Set nail heads with a nail set if needed.

PHOTO I The last few rows will need to be installed by hand nailing the same way the first few rows were installed. At the final row, use a pry bar to force the boards tightly together. Be sure to protect the wall with a thin wood block before prying.

8 Position and nail courses until you get to the final row, remembering to leave a ½ in. expansion gap at walls and where the wood flooring meets other flooring materials **(See Photo H).** In almost all cases, you'll need to do some trimming and planning to work around obstructions in the floor or turns and changes in the floorplan (See *Working Around Obstructions,* previous page). Continue to loosely arrange boards for seven or eight courses at a time to plan a balanced and properly staggered seam arrangement and to make best use of flooring material.

9 Position boards to fit in the last row. Insert a pry bar between each board and the wall (protect the wall with a thin piece of scrap) and push sideways against the pry bar, forcing the joint closed. Drill pilot holes and face-nail the board at every joist, halfway between joists and within 2 in. of the board ends **(See Photo I)** as you did on the first row of boards.

10 Install a reducing strip at doorways or other areas where the wood flooring meets a lower flooring surface (See page 58). Reducing strips will fit over a tongue or square against grooved ends and are available in several thicknesses. Attach a threshold when the two surfaces are basically level. Unless you're installing prefinished flooring, sand the surface of the floor to even out any ridges or rough areas, then apply the floor finish (See page 67). Install base trim.

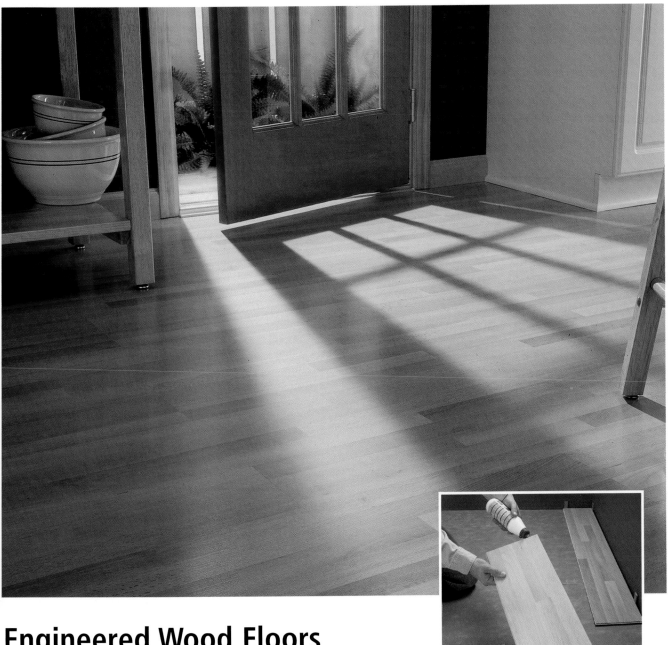

Engineered Wood Floors

Engineered wood flooring systems have made a huge impact in the do-it-yourself home flooring market in recent years. Advances in quality, appearance and ease of installation are the primary reasons behind their explosion in popularity. More manufacturers now are entering this product market and, as a result, the relative cost has decreased to the point that these systems can be cheaper to install than traditional oak, maple or pine solid wood flooring.

Engineered wood flooring products are man-made formulations created by applying veneer or wood-grain plastic laminate to a wood-based substrate. Where standard tongue-and-groove flooring is ¾ in. thick, most engineered wood floor panels are only ⅜ in. thick, making them easier to handle and more

economical to produce. The most common engineered wood floors frequently are referred to as "floating floors" because they are not nailed down or otherwise attached to the subfloor. Instead, they "float" on an underlayment pad and are bonded to one another with glued tongue-and-groove joints. In most cases, they can be installed with simple shop tools just about every handyman or weekender already owns.

The main differences between engineered wood flooring products are in the material used for the pattern layer and the body of the product. The more expensive products usually have a layer of real wood veneer on top, laminated to a body composed of three ⅛-in.-thick plywood plies. Typically, they are prefinished with a hard, polymerized topcoat or a laminated wear layer. The more common products these days, however, feature a pattern layer of plastic laminate with a printed pattern, generally a wood grain. The "topcoat" is usually a wear layer of high-tech material such as clear melamine. The body of most mass-market engineered flooring products is made of particleboard or medium-density fiberboard (MDF). Some products also feature a laminate backing to discourage moisture penetration from below.

Most manufacturers offer a selection of underlayment pads, typically made of various grades of foam. Sheets of plastic moisture barrier also are available for installations over concrete. Glues, trim pieces and some specialty installation tools also are offered by the flooring system manufacturer.

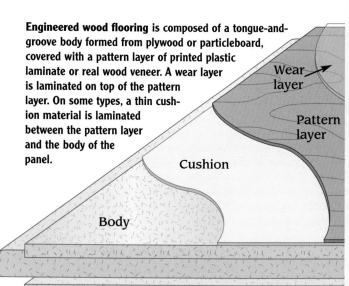

Engineered wood flooring is composed of a tongue-and-groove body formed from plywood or particleboard, covered with a pattern layer of printed plastic laminate or real wood veneer. A wear layer is laminated on top of the pattern layer. On some types, a thin cushion material is laminated between the pattern layer and the body of the panel.

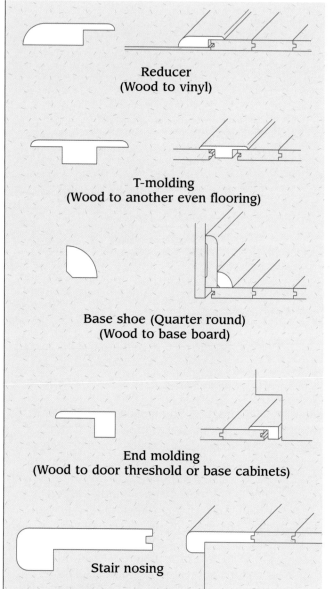

Reducer
(Wood to vinyl)

T-molding
(Wood to another even flooring)

Base shoe (Quarter round)
(Wood to base board)

End molding
(Wood to door threshold or base cabinets)

Stair nosing

Transition moldings for floating floors are used to bridge gaps between adjoining floor surfaces and between the floors and walls or base cabinets. Specific products vary by manufacturer.

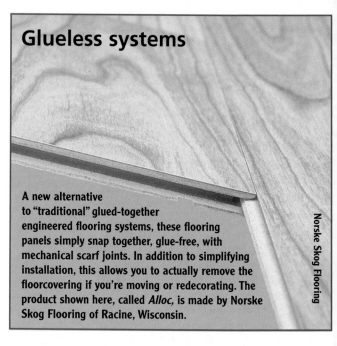

Glueless systems

A new alternative to "traditional" glued-together engineered flooring systems, these flooring panels simply snap together, glue-free, with mechanical scarf joints. In addition to simplifying installation, this allows you to actually remove the floorcovering if you're moving or redecorating. The product shown here, called *Alloc*, is made by Norske Skog Flooring of Racine, Wisconsin.

Norske Skog Flooring

Installing & maintaining engineered wood floors

- Let the flooring panels acclimate in the project room for two or three days before installing them.

- When ordering floorboards, add 10 to 15% to the total square footage of the room to allow for waste.

- Install a vapor barrier before beneath the underlayment pad if the subfloor is concrete—even if you're installing the flooring over another floorcovering.

- Clean surfaces with a vacuum cleaner (non-beater) then damp-mop with warm water. Avoid strong detergents and any abrasive cleaners.

- Always use protective pads on the bottoms of furniture legs to prevent scratching.

"Floating" floors

"Floating" floors are wood-based floor systems where the panels are bonded to one another, but not to the floor, so they "float" on a pad-type underlayment. Read the floor system manufacturer's directions carefully before you begin the installation. Specific steps required for the product you choose may vary from the how-to sequence that follows.

1 Determine the flooring direction you want and choose the longest wall parallel to this direction as the starting wall. One of the advantages of floating floor systems is that you don't need to orient the floorboards so they're perpendicular to the floor joists, as you do with a nail-down floor.

2 Cut and install strips of foam pad perpendicular to the flooring direction. *NOTE: In most cases, you'll want to purchase the pad, glue and transition fittings from the manufacturer of your engineered*

PHOTO A Roll out the foam-pad underlayment so the seams are butted together and perpendicular to the direction of the flooring panels. Tape the seams together to keep the underlayment from shifting.

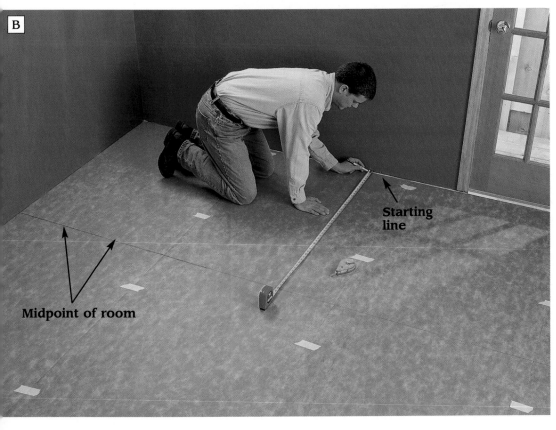

Starting line

Midpoint of room

PHOTO B Draw a reference line that establishes the midpoint of the room, parallel to the wall at which you'll begin the installation. Measure out an equal distance from the reference line at several points and mark points within about ½ in. of the starting wall. Connect the marked points with a chalkline to create a starting line for the first row of flooring panels. The starting line should be exactly parallel to the midpoint reference line. If the wall is out of square, the gap between the starting line and the wall should accommodate the difference.

PHOTO C Begin by installing a complete row of panels along the starting wall. To reinforce the tongue-and-groove joints, squirt a healthy dab of glue into the groove then slip the grooved panel over the mating tongue. Press the boards together tightly.

PHOTO D After forming the end-seams between panels within a row, rap the open end of the last full panel with a mallet and hammer block to force the joint together tightly. The hammer block is made by trimming the tongue off the end of a cutoff piece of flooring material.

floorboards—failing to do this may invalidate the product warranty. Secure each strip in place with masking tape **(See Photo A),** butting the edges together.

3 Mark the midpoints of the walls that are perpendicular to the flooring direction and snap a chalkline between the midpoints as a reference for locating the center of the room. Every few feet along the starting wall, measure and mark equal distances from this centerline to within roughly ½ in. of the starting wall **(See Photo B).** Snap a chalkline between the marks. This line is used as a guide for aligning the first row of flooring boards, ensuring that the boards in the center of the room look square to the walls, even if the room is not square. Base trim will be installed to conceal the gaps between the flooring and the walls after the flooring installation is finished.

4 Dry-lay the first row of panels, aligning the grooved edges of the first row of boards against the starting line marked near the starting wall. Use scrap wood shims to maintain the ½-in. expansion gap between the flooring and the walls (if your walls aren't perfectly straight, you'll need to vary the thicknesses of the individual shims). Use full-length floorboard panels, trimming only the last panel in the row for length.

5 After dry-laying the row, separate the panels. Apply plenty of glue to the mating ends of the panels **(See Photo C).** Most manufacturers specify what kind of glue to use, how much to use and whether to apply it to the groove or the tongue on their product— make certain to check the manufacturer's instructions before you start. Interlock the ends of the first two panels in the row. Use a hammer block (a scrap piece of flooring about 1 ft. long with the tongue cut off) and a mallet to

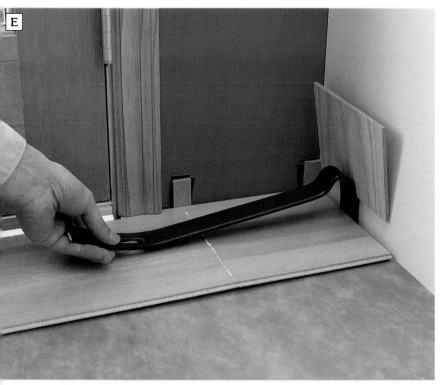

PHOTO E With a piece of scrap protecting the wall, wedge the curved claw of a flat pry bar between the end panel and the wall, then twist the pry bar with sideways pressure to force the panel back against the previous panel. Insert a spacer between the panel and the wall before removing the pry bar.

PHOTO F After the first row of panels is glued together, dry-lay the next four or five rows to test the fit. This will also allow you to make more efficient use of the flooring material, with a little trial and error.

drive the board tight against the adjacent board **(See Photo D).** Remove any excess glue that squeezes out with a damp cloth. Check to make sure the spacers between the flooring panels and the wall are in correct position. Continue end-joining panels until the row is completed

6 Insert a pry bar between the last panel in the row and the wall (protect the wall with a thin piece of scrap) and push sideways on the pry bar to force the panel firmly against the end of the adjoining panel **(See Photo E).** Slip a spacer between the end of the last panel and the wall to keep the seam tight.

NOTE: The moisture in the glue will cause the edges of the panels to raise slightly at the seams. As the glue continues to dry and the moisture levels in the boards equalize, the ridges caused by the raised edges will flatten back down. This may take a few weeks.

Starter Wall

LAYOUT SEQUENCE: Although the visible surfaces of most engineered wood floor panels are composed of multiple "boards" of varying length, you'll generally get the best visual results if you stagger the panels at one end of the room. Make the first panel in the first row a full panel; then, cut the first panel in the second row to one-third length; use the cut-off two-thirds of this panel to begin the third row.

How to install a "floating" floor (continued)

PHOTO G Cut and trim panels to fit during the dry-lay stage of the installation. For fitting around outside corners and cabinets, fashion a template from cardboard, then use the template to trace the cutout shape onto a panel.

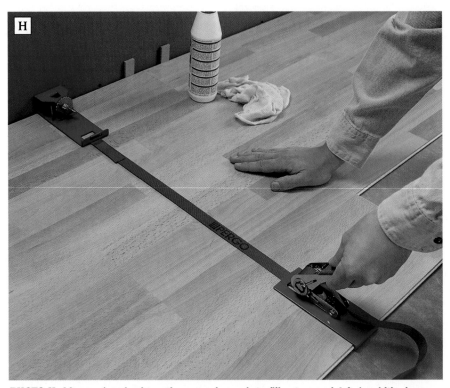

PHOTO H After you've glued together enough panels to fill out around 4 ft. in width, draw the panels together at several points along the rows to tighten the tongue-and-groove joints. Make sure to do this before the glue has set up (a typical "open time" for glue is around 20 to 30 minutes). The specialty strap clamp shown above is produced by the *Pergo* flooring manufacturing company for use with their product.

7 To start the second row, most engineered flooring manufacturers suggest that you cut the first panel so the end seams in the rows will be staggered. *Pergo,* the manufacturer of the system being installed here, recommends that you cut the first panel in the second row to one-third length, then use a two-thirds length panel to begin the third row. Repeat the full-⅓-⅔ sequence beginning with the fourth row (See illustration, previous page). Following your stagger pattern, dry-lay the next four to six rows of panels **(See Photo F).** Cut panels as needed to fit around obstructions, corners and cabinets (See *Working Around Obstructions,* page 55). Leave a ½-in. expansion gap between the panels and any permanent obstructions **(See Photo G).**

8 Separate the dry-laid panels, then begin gluing them back together in order, starting with the first panel in the second row. Specific gluing techniques vary by manufacturer: we applied glue to the grooved panel at each joint, then pressed the tongue of the adjoining panel into the groove. Use the hammer block and mallet to seat each panel tightly against the adjoining panel.

9 Finish installing panels in this row, and continue installing four to six full rows. At this point, some manufacturers recommend that you use a device to draw the installed panels together tightly. *Pergo* manufactures strap clamps with custom clamp heads **(See Photo H).** You'll need several of these clamps for an average-sized room. Take care not to over-tighten the clamps, and leave them in place until the glue has set completely. If you can't locate special clamps, an alternate method we've found to be effective is to press the panels together tightly and apply masking tape over the seams at short intervals **(See Photo I-Option).** But whenever possible, follow the manufacturer's recommendations precisely.

10 Install subsequent panels in groups of four to six rows, dry-laying each group completely to make sure the panels fit before gluing the panels together.

11 When you reach the opposite wall of the room from the starting wall, position panels to fit in the last row so a ½-in. expansion gap remains. If you're lucky, the panels in the last row will be the correct width. But more likely, you'll need to rip-cut them to width. If you have a table saw, use it to rip the panels for this row. Otherwise, a circular saw with a straightedge cutting guide may be used. Whichever tool you use, cut so the rotation of the saw blade is down into the surface of each panel to prevent tear-out from the saw blade. Test-fit the last row, then apply glue to each panel and push into position, inserting a pry bar between the panel and the wall (protect the wall with a thin piece of scrap) and pushing sideways against the pry bar, forcing the panel tight against the adjacent piece **(See Photo J).** Clamp or tape the last rows to hold them together until the glue sets. Any dried glue residue should be removable with warm water, but check the glue container for recommendations.

12 In most cases, you'll need to install reducing strips or other transition trim somewhere in the installation area. A sampling of these pieces is shown in the illustration on page 58. You'll definitely need to install a threshold or transition strip in any doorway leading from the project room to an adjoining room. In some cases, you will be able to find moldings that have the same color and pattern as the flooring panels, but in other cases you'll need to use coordinating trim. Since each manufacturer produces slightly different trim types, work with your flooring salesperson to determine which products you need.

PHOTO I (OPTION) It's been our experience that the better-made floor system products fit together well enough that they can be held together with adequate pressure using masking tape instead of clamps. But if you choose to use this method, be aware that it may not conform to the manufacturer's suggested installation techniques and using it may have implications on your product warranty.

PHOTO J Force the panels in the final row against the panel in the neighboring row using a flat pry bar. Slip spacers between the panels and the wall once each tongue-and-groove joint is forced together tightly.

VARIATION: How to glue down strip flooring

PHOTO A Attach a guide strip parallel to the center of the room about 30 in. from the wall.

PHOTO B Apply flooring adhesive in a small section, then set the first row against the guide strip, gluing the ends together as you go.

PHOTO C Install the rest of the floorboards in groups of three or four rows at a time, dry-laying all the boards in each group before you apply the adhesive. Glue end seams only. Use a hammer block and mallet to drive the boards together tightly.

Glued-down wood floors

Engineered-wood strip flooring (usually ⅜ to ½ in. thick) can be glued directly to the subfloor. Use the adhesive specified by the flooring manufacturer.

1 Mark a center reference line in the middle of the room *(See Photo B, page 52)* then measure from that line toward the starting wall and mark points equidistant from the centerline that are about 30 in. from the starting wall. Attach a 1 × 2 guide strip flush against this line **(See Photo A).** You will stand in this narrow area to begin the installation, and the strip keeps the first rows of boards straight and in position while you're working. Before continuing, dry-lay the first three or four rows of boards, cutting them as needed to fit. For best results, stagger the lengths of the first board in each row (See page 61). Remove the boards, keeping them in order.

2 Spread adhesive onto the subfloor outside the strip, enough for 3 or 4 rows of boards, using a notched trowel (See page 34). Position the first floorboard so the end is about ½ in. from the wall and the tongue side is against the guide strip. Set the board into the adhesive, keeping the edge flush against the guide strip. Apply wood glue to the end of the next board and press it against the first board to make the tongue-and-groove joint joining the ends **(See Photo B).** Make sure the second board is also tight against the guide strip. Wipe off excess glue.

3 Install all the boards in the first row, then install the second row, working away from the guide strip. Make sure to leave the ½-in. expansion gap at walls. Only apply wood glue to the end joints, not to the joined edges. After positioning each board, rap it tightly against the board or boards in the previous row with a mallet and hammer block (a scrap of flooring with the tongue cut off). Continue spreading adhesive and installing boards until you reach the opposite wall **(See Photo C).** Cut boards to fit around obstacles and corners as you dry-lay each group of three or four rows (See page 55).

4 Remove the 1 × 2 strip and complete the installation up to the wall—you'll likely need to rip-cut boards to fit along one or both parallel walls. Seat the floorboards securely in the adhesive by rolling the entire floor with a 100-pound flooring roller within 3 hours of spreading the first section of adhesive **(See Photo D).**

PHOTO D After all the floorboards are installed (but no more than three hours after the first section of adhesive is applied) roll the floor surface with a flooring roller. Where possible, roll across the long seams at a slightly diagonal direction.

Parquet flooring

Installing a parquet engineered wood floor is more like installing a vinyl or ceramic tile floor than a wood floor. Simply divide the work area into square quadrants and lay the tile in small sections, following the layout lines. Use a hammer block (See Step 3, previous page) and mallet to drive the tiles together, but don't drive too hard since only the adhesive is holding them to the floor. Whether the tiles are 6 × 6 or 12 × 12 in., they'll have tongue-and-groove shapes on all four sides so you can create a tight layout. Roll with a flooring roller once the installation is complete.

Create layout lines for parquet flooring the same way you would for ceramic or vinyl tile (See pages 30 to 31). Apply adhesive with a notched trowel, taking care not to obscure the layout lines, and lay the tile in small, square sections (left photo). Always make a dry-run of each section before applying the adhesive, and cut tiles as needed during the dry-run. When you're done, roll the floor with a flooring roller (right photo).

Removing an old wood floor surface then sanding the floorboards thoroughly and applying a finish gives new life to a dingy old floor. It is one of the most common do-it-yourself remodeling projects.

Before

Refinishing Wood Floors

Sanding and refinishing a wood floor is a project most do-it-yourselfers will attempt at some point. The process is loud and messy, but with the help of powerful floor sanding equipment, you don't need to be a pro to get the job done. There is a big difference, however, between getting it done and getting it done well. The most common mistake we make is to be so amazed by the fact that the old finish is gone and fresh wood is exposed that we neglect to follow up the initial resurfacing with adequate finish sanding. The result is a floor that's riddled with sanding marks and dips, as well as the telltale border ridges that show quite clearly where you switched from the drum sander to a disc sander or edger.

The lesson most people learn after they finish their first floor-sanding project is that sanding a floor is really a two-stage process: first, you remove the old finish by resurfacing with coarse-grit papers; then, the actual sanding of the floorboards begins.

Evaluating your floor

Before you begin a floor sanding project, check your existing floor to make sure it is a good candidate for refinishing. Here are a few things to look for:

• *Type of flooring.* Obviously, only wood floors can be sanded and refinished. But not every wood floor will take sanding. *Engineered wood floors* with wood veneer or laminate top layers cannot be sanded. Engineered floors with a solid wood top lamination at least 1/8 in. thick may be sanded, but it is risky. *Parquet floors* generally can be sanded, provided the strips that make up the parquet tiles are solid wood (as a rule, use finer sanding grits and work diagonally across the field area). *Solid wood floors* a full ¾ in. in thickness are the most suitable for sanding.

• *Condition of floor.* Regardless of type, floors must meet certain condition requirements to be suitable for sanding. *Levelness:* A wood floor with a gradual slope doesn't present any particular problems for refinishing. But if the floor contains numerous dips or rises of more than ⅛ in. in a small area, you will have difficulty sanding it with a drum-style floor sander. Larger sanders cannot follow undulations in the floor, and the only way for you to sand the finish off will be to go over and over the problem area until the high areas are reduced to the height of the lower areas. Not only is this a lot of work, but you'll quite possibly sand deeply enough into the higher boards to expose the tongue of the joint between boards. You can use power hand sanders (in particular, belt sanders and random-orbit sanders) to sand an uneven floor, but it is quite time consuming.

• *Thickness of floorboards.* Every time a floor is sanded, it will typically lose between 1⁄32 and 1⁄16 in. of top surface. Therefore, it is not wise to sand any floor that has been resurfaced multiple times TIP: *To see the ends of the floorboards so you can evaluate how much of the surface is left, remove any vent or duct grates in the floor and inspect the ends of the trimmed boards.*

• *Condition of subfloor.* If the subfloor is weak or has detectable bounce, you'll have a hard time getting a smooth finish with a drum sander. The tool produces extreme vibrations as it sands and any bounce in the floor will cause the sanding drum to chatter.

Power Floor Sanders

The *drum sander* is the workhorse used to complete just about every floor sanding project. Available for rent by the hour or the day at most rental centers and many hardware stores, they are powerful sanding tools that can resurface a floor in a hurry. *Edgers* (disc sanders) and sanding papers are also obtained from the rental center.

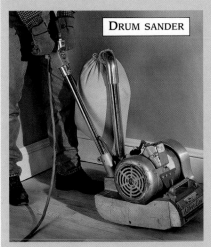

DRUM SANDER

A drum sander does most of the hard work on a typical floor refinishing project.

EDGER

An edger is a powerful disc sander used in areas the drum sander can't reach.

Installing sanding belts on the sanding drum can be a real test of patience. But take the time to learn to do it correctly, since you'll be changing the belts quite frequently. Check that the belt is oriented in the right direction (there are usually arrows printed on the back of the belt) and make sure the belt is tight and the ends are securely fastened in the slots and there are no ridges or bumps. A poorly installed sanding belt will virtually disintegrate when you turn the sander on. Unplug the sander before changing belts.

DRUM SANDER BELTS

A   B   C   D

Sanding belts and discs are often the most expensive material in a floor refinishing project. Get plenty of them when you rent your sanders—you can always return what you don't use. In most cases you'll need: (A) fine (100 grit); (B) medium fine (80 grit); (C) medium (60 grit); and (D) coarse (36 grit).

Preparing for the project

• Scrape off adhesive and residue from old floorcoverings, using a floor scraper.

• Remove everything from the room, including drapes and wall decorations; seal off vents with plastic (turn off heat or air conditioning first) and remove any floor registers; drape light fixtures with plastic (trash bags work well).

• Make any necessary floor repairs (See pages 72 to 75) and fasten down any loose boards by face nailing into joists and subflooring at an angle with flooring or finish nails. Make certain to countersink these and any other protruding nailheads so they're at least ⅛ in. below the flooring surface. Also remove any staples or other objects in the floor that will rip the sandpaper on the sanders—locking pliers are a good tool for staple removal.

• Vacuum the floor to remove dust and debris.

• Remove the base shoe molding throughout the room. To limit the chance of breaking old molding, drive the nails through the trim boards with a nailset (See photo below).

Drive nailheads through old base shoe to make it easier to remove.

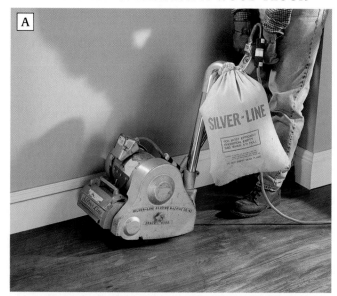

PHOTO A Start at the right side of the room, a few inches away from the wall that's parallel to the floorboards. Back up against the wall behind you. With the drum sander tipped back so the sanding drum is not contacting the floor, turn the sander on. Once the drum is spinning at full speed, slowly roll the sander forward, lowering the drum, until the drum engages the floor.

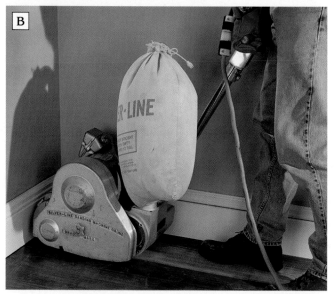

PHOTO B As you near the wall at the end of the pass, begin to lift up on the floor sander, slowly disengaging the drum from contact with the floor. Roll the sander back to the starting point, watching out for the power cord. Do not attempt to sand as you move backwards, and take care not to let the sander tip forward while the sanding drum is spinning.

PHOTO C Begin the second sanding pass with the sander positioned so the drum overlaps about half of the area sanded in the first pass. Continue this overlap approach throughout the project.

Refinishing floors

Read the section on evaluating your floors (Pages 66 to 67) before beginning your project to make sure your floor is suitable for sanding. Also read and follow the "Preparing for the project" information on the previous page. And ask for a demonstration (or at least written instructional material) at the rental center where you obtain the sanding equipment.

Wear ear and eye protection, gloves, sturdy shoes, long pants and a particle mask when operating power sanding equipment.

If you've never operated a floor sander before, start sanding in the least visible part of the room. Or, you can even lay an old sheet of plywood down on the floor and practice sanding on it first (make sure the edge of the plywood behind you is pressed against a wall).

PHOTO D After making sanding passes all the way to the opposite wall from the starting wall, reverse direction and sand back in the direction of the starting wall. After all of the old finish is removed, switch to finer grit belts and repeat the process. Each finer grit will remove the sanding marks left by the previous, coarser-grit belt.

1 Install a sanding belt in the floor sander (See page 67). Try one of the medium-grit belts first: the goal being to identify the finest grit you can use and still have the resurfacing go fairly quickly. A 60-grit belt is a good place to start. The initial pass with the sander should remove at least half of the finish, exposing raw wood. If the 60-grit belt is not removing half the finish or is gumming up quickly with old finish, switch to a coarser grit (36 or even 20 grit in extreme cases).

2 The best place to begin sanding is at the wall parallel to the flooring direction on the right side of the room. Start with the sander just a few inches away from the wall. Back up against the wall next to the starting wall **(See Photo A).** Tilt the machine handle back to lift the sanding drum off the floor. Turn on the machine. Lower the sanding head as you begin to move forward—the sanding drum should be moving forward as it

contacts the floor, otherwise it will gouge the wood.

3 Once the sander engages the floor, the rotation of the sanding drum will exert quite a bit of force, pulling you forward. Rather than pushing the sander forward, you make progress by restraining the sander, allowing it to creep forward at a relatively slow pace. This is one part of floor sanding that takes a bit of practice to develop a "feel." Move forward with the sander. When you are one to two feet away from the opposite wall, begin to rock the sander back, gradually disengaging the drum from the floor **(See Photo B).** Most floor sanders have bumpers on the leading edge to prevent damage to the walls and baseboard, but avoid hitting the wall with too much force. **IMPORTANT: Never stop the forward progress of the sander while the drum is contacting the floor—it takes only a fraction of a second to create a visible gouge.**

4 Keep the sanding drum above the floor, move the cord out of the way and pull the machine backward to the starting point (cord management is an important part of floor-sanding safety: always be aware of the position of the cord, but pay particular attention when you're backing up the machine). Move the sander over so the drum overlaps about half of the first pass, then make another pass in the same manner **(See Photo C).**

5 Continue making passes until reaching the other side of the room—make the last pass as close to the left wall as possible. Then, turn the machine around and sand in the opposite direction, removing the surfacing that was under your feet when you started each pass **(See Photo D).** Stop the machine to change the dust bag when it gets half-full. Also change sandpaper if it clogs or wears to the point where it isn't aggressively removing material.

PHOTO E Use an edger to remove the finish around the perimeter of the room where the floor sander will not reach.

PHOTO F Scrape finish at the corners and under radiators with a sharp floor scraper or a power detail sander.

6 Continue to sand the floor with the coarser grit belts until all of the old finish that can be reached by the floor sander is gone. Since most floor sanders are rented by the hour, the most economical way to proceed is to continue sanding the general floor area with finer grit belts, vacuuming the floor to remove wood dust and debris each time you change grits (if not more frequently). For most floors, sanding up to 100 grit will yield a sufficiently smooth surface that takes a finish well. After you've done all you can with the floor sander, return it to the rental store and replace it with an edger (a powerful disc sander). NOTE: At this point the exposed wood floor is very vulnerable. Do not walk on it with dirty shoes and do not contact it with bare feet or hands: the oil in your skin will fill the wood pores so they do not take finish like the rest of the floor, and you'll end up with a permanent shadow of a footprint or hand print on your floor. Spreading a clean, dry tarp over the sanded floor is an excellent precaution.

7 Using a coarse-grit sanding disc, remove the old finish

PHOTO G (OPTION) After all the floor sanding is complete, give the surface a final pre-finish "clean-up" with a sanding screen mounted to a floor buffer, then buff with a buffing pad.

around the perimeter of the room with the edger. The main purpose of the edger is to remove finish and wood in the areas where the floor sander would not reach so those areas are flat and level with the rest of the floor **(See Photo E).** Tilt the edger back before start-

ing, making sure it has reached full speed before sandpaper contacts the floor. Move the edger counter-clockwise around the room. Because disc sanders sand in a circular path, they will leave more scratches than the floor sander, so switch up to a finer grit as soon as you can. Then, unless you're very experienced with the edger, finish-sand the floor and blend in the areas where the floor sander meets the edger using a hand-held power sander (a random orbit sander is best).

8 Even after all that power sanding, you'll still find that there are a few corners and nooks you just couldn't reach. The traditional method to take care of these is with a very sharp floor scraper **(See Photo F).** But if you're a stickler for power sanders, you can use a detail sander with a triangular sanding pad instead.

OPTION: Prepare the sanded floor for the finish application by buffing it with a floor buffer, using a sanding screen and then buffing pads **(See Photo G).**

9 After sanding is completed, remove sawdust from walls, window ledges and trim, then thoroughly vacuum the floor. Remove dust residue with a tack cloth, or damp rag if using water-based finish.

10 Apply wood stain, if you plan on using it (we chose not to). Then, apply the first coat of finish (usually thinned slightly) to seal the floor, following the manufacturer's directions. We used a sleeve-type paint pad with an extension pole to apply the material **(See Photo H).** Work with the grain as much as you can. Stroke in one direction and don't go back over finish that has begun to set. Let the seal coat dry.

11 Use a floor polisher with a fine abrasive screen to smooth irregularities left by dust or air bubbles after each coat of finish dries **(See Photo I).** Vacuum and wipe dust from the floor after buffing. Then apply at least three thin coats of topcoat for a durable surface **(See Photo J).** Reattach base shoe moldings.

PHOTO H The first coat of top-coat product should be thinned. For ease of application, we poured the finish onto the floor with a plastic watering can, then spread it out with the grain using a special staining sleeve and pole designed for use with floors.

PHOTO I After each coat of finish has dried, buff the surface with a fine buffing pad to remove surface imperfections caused by trapped air bubbles or small particles. Vacuum the dust, then wipe down with a damp cloth before applying the next coat of finish.

PHOTO J Apply at least three thin coats of topcoat product, not one or two thick coats. Follow the finish manufacturer's application instructions carefully. Let the finish cure for several days before allowing traffic on the floor.

Remove dark stains from floorboards with two-part wood bleach. You'll need to sand the stained area first to remove the wood finish. Then, blend the bleach components together and apply to the stained wood with a brush, following the manufacturer's instructions. It may take several applications to lighten the stain. When you're done bleaching the wood, apply white vinegar to the area to neutralize the acid in the bleach. Sand down any raised wood grain, then apply finish, blending and feathering the new finish into the old, if necessary.

Repairing Wood Floors

Occasional scratches and dents are to be expected with just about any type of wood floor. Many common problems, including dark stains, scratches, holes and larger localized damage, can be remedied with one of the repairs shown here.

Replacing floorboards

When flooring damage cannot be rectified with minor repairs, replace damaged boards with strips or planks of identical wood. If you're fortunate, you'll have a few extra pieces of the original floorboards in your basement or closet. Otherwise, purchase new materials that are as close to matching as you can find (building materials salvage yards are a good source if the flooring is fairly old). If you can't find well matched material, or don't want to buy an entire carton of flooring just to replace a small section of a single board, another option is to remove a few floorboards from a less visible area, such as a closet, then replace the removed boards with near-matching boards.

HOW TO REPAIR DEEP SCRATCHES, SMALL HOLES & DENTS

1 Clean the area around the damage thoroughly and remove any loose splinters. Fill the scratch or hole with stainable wood putty. Overfill slightly, then sand the patch back after the putty dries so it's level with the surrounding floor surface.

2 On a piece of flooring or scrap wood of the same species, apply a few dabs of putty. Let the putty dry then sand it lightly. Experiment with stains and touch-up products to find one that matches your floor finish when applied to the putty. Apply the matching finish over the putty patch with a cotton swab.

1 Determine the patch area, planning adjacent end seams so they are at least 6 in. apart. Plan an irregular sequence of end seams that matches the existing flooring pattern. TIP: *It's better to remove more flooring so the patched area blends in well than to try and save on time and wood.* Outline the patch area with masking tape, then score along the crosscut lines using a utility knife and square, unless you are removing a piece at its original end seam **(See Photo A)**.

2 Drill series of overlapping holes that touch the insides of the scored lines (or end seams) in the patch area, using a ½-in.-dia. spade bit **(See Photo B)**. Drill only deep enough to cut all the way through the floorboard.

3 Set a circular saw blade so the cutting depth is equal to the flooring thickness. On an outside board in the patch area, make two parallel cuts near the center of the board, connecting the holes drilled at the ends **(See Photo C)**.

4 Use a flat pry bar to lever out the pieces. Don't pry against good flooring boards. Once this first board is removed, use the pry bar to lever out the remaining boards in the patch area **(See Photo D)**. A cat's paw may be helpful for removing nails. Where the tongue of a damaged board fits in a groove of a good board, use a chisel to split the tongue off the damaged board before removing the board **(See Photo E)**. Carefully work the tongue remnant from the groove—a small chisel may help in cutting the tongue into small pieces. Then pry the nails out, again being careful not to damage the groove.

5 Square up the ends where you have drilled holes using a sharp chisel **(See Photo F)**. Face the beveled edge of the chisel toward the repair area.

HOW TO REPLACE DAMAGED FLOORBOARDS

PHOTO A Outline the repair area with masking tape. If you plan to crosscut damaged boards, plan the cuts so the new boards will be staggered by at least 6 in. at the end seams.

PHOTO B Drill ½-in. dia. holes at the scored crosscut lines to "cut" the boards or board sections that need to be removed. Overlap the holes.

PHOTO C Set your circular saw cutting depth to equal to the thickness of the floorboards, then make a pair of parallel cuts connecting the rows of holes at each end of each board. This splits the board so it can be removed more easily.

PHOTO D
Remove the damaged floorboard or floorboards with a flat pry bar.

PHOTO E If one of the damaged floorboards forms the tongue portion of a tongue-and-groove joint with an undamaged board, insert a wood chisel into the seam and drive it with a mallet to splinter off the tongue from the damaged board.

PHOTO F
Square off the ends of boards that were "cut" by drilling overlapping holes, using a sharp wood chisel. For a straight face, make sure the bevel side of the chisel is facing away from the board being trimmed.

6 Install a new floorboard on the side of the patch where there is a tongue on the existing good board **(See Photo G).** Use a scrap piece of flooring as a hammer block to make certain the board fits tightly against the good board so the seams line up. Shim the board so it is flush with the good board, if necessary, with pieces of 15-pound building felt. Blind-nail with 8d finish or spiral shank nails at a 45° angle through the tongue, at joist locations. Drill pilot holes for the nails. (See page 54 for more information.)

7 Continue installing floorboards in the patch area, lining up the seams so the new flooring boards match those of the surrounding floorboards. Place a new board on the subfloor and slide it into position when it fits between two existing boards. If you don't have access to slide a board into position, cut off the bottom lip of the grooves on the board and the end tongue, if present. Use a table saw **(See Photo H, inset)** or a circular saw with the blade set to the appropriate depth and a straight-edge guide.

8 Insert the tongue of the new board into the groove of the existing board, then push the new board into place **(See Photo H).** The remaining top lip of the groove on the new board fits over the tongue on the adjacent board.

9 Face nail any board where you can't blind nail through the tongue. Drill angled pilot holes at the ends and at the joists, about ½ in. from the edges of the board **(See Photo I).** Set the nails below the board surface and fill holes with stainable wood putty.

10 Mask off old flooring with tape, then finish the patched area to match the existing flooring **(See Photo J).** Tint wood putty prior to finishing (See page 72).

PHOTO G Set the first replacement board into position, then blind nail it to the subfloor with 8d finish or spiral-shank nails. You'll need to drill pilot holes for the nails. Set the nailheads with a nailset.

PHOTO H To fit a board between two installed boards, trim the bottom lip of the grooved edge off (inset photo), then install.

PHOTO I Boards that can't be accessed for blind-nailing are face nailed near the ends. Set the nailheads and fill them with putty. Also face-nail near end seams that are butted together without a tongue-and-groove joint.

PHOTO J Stain the patch boards to match the existing floor (See page 72). You may need to tint wood putty in nail holes before staining the patched area. Topcoat to match, blending and feathering as best you can to match the finish in the rest of the room.

Resilient Flooring

Resilient flooring is a versatile flooring type offering a wide variety of colors, patterns and styles in a range of relatively inexpensive products made essentially from vinyl. It can resemble ceramic tile, natural stone or wood floors, provide a bold geometric design or bring striking color into a room. The combination of ease of installation, durability and low cost make it a popular home improvement material.

Resilient vinyl flooring is available in two basic product types, sheet vinyl and vinyl tiles. Sheet vinyl is purchased by the lineal foot off of 6- or 12-ft.-wide rolls and is either full-spread-bonded or perimeter-bonded to the floor underlayment. Full-spread means adhesive is spread over the entire underlayment surface. This takes longer to do but creates a more durable installation. In a perimeter-bond installation, adhesive is spread only around the edges of the room and underneath seams. Perimeter-bond is installed very quickly but is more likely to come loose. The lack of seams in a sheet vinyl installation makes it attractive in rooms where moisture is common, such as bathrooms, kitchens and laundry rooms.

Vinyl tiles, usually available in 12×12-in. squares, are either *dry-back* or *self-adhesive.* Dry-back tiles require spreading of adhesive underneath them. Generally, these tiles form an extremely durable and inexpensive floorcovering. A paper backing protects the adhesive on self-adhesive tiles and is removed just prior to positioning and setting on the underlayment. This is the easiest type of all flooring products to install, but the adhesive on self-adhesive tiles does not form as durable a bond as spread adhesive.

The thickness of vinyl flooring is a good gauge of quality since thicker vinyl flooring contains more vinyl. Solid vinyl is the most expensive type. The color and pattern run throughout the flooring. Vinyl composition flooring has less vinyl, which is combined with non-vinyl fillers to create the design. The color and pattern on printed vinyl flooring is printed on a very thin non-vinyl layer that is bonded to a layer of urethane and vinyl to provide durability. Check with a flooring dealer for advice on the best vinyl-flooring product for your project.

Always use the adhesive recommended by the manufacturer under vinyl flooring. Besides risking flooring failure, using the wrong adhesive usually voids the product warranty. Don't attempt to use additional adhesive on self-adhesive tiles to strengthen the bond because chemicals in the two types of adhesive may react to ruin the flooring. Keep the project area well ventilated when spreading adhesives because many adhesives produce harmful vapors.

Resilient flooring types

Adhesive-backed vinyl tiles are peel-and-stick products offering great economy and easy installation (pages 79 to 83).

Dry-back vinyl tiles are set into a bed of flooring adhesive. Generally, they are more durable than self-adhesive types (pages 84 to 87).

Sheet vinyl is a preferred floor covering for wet areas because it is a seamless product in many installations, making it impervious to moisture (pages 90 to 91).

Designing a tile layout

Use graph paper to plan a layout for a border or other geometric pattern. This will prevent positioning a tile incorrectly during installation and make it easier to order the correct amounts of the various tiles. Measure the room's dimensions and transfer them to the paper using a scale of ¼ in. equals 1 ft. Include the position of outside corners and any cabinets or other large obstacles that will affect the placement of the pattern.

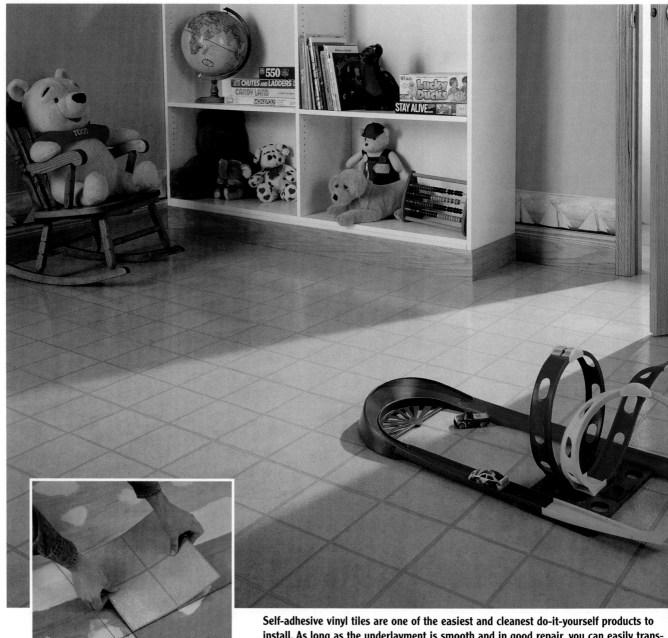

Self-adhesive vinyl tiles are one of the easiest and cleanest do-it-yourself products to install. As long as the underlayment is smooth and in good repair, you can easily transform a room in a single afternoon with these inexpensive floorcovering products.

Self-adhesive vinyl tiles

Anyone looking for an inexpensive floorcovering product that's easy and clean to install should start the search with self-adhesive vinyl tiles. Known also as "sticky-backs," these 12 × 12-in. tiles are bonded directly to the floor underlayment after the peel-off backing is removed. As long as the underlayment is perfectly smooth and your layout lines are square, you can achieve professional-looking results in a hurry with these DIY-friendly products.

It's a general rule in home remodeling that the products that are cheapest and easiest to install aren't usually the most long-lasting. This is also true of self-adhesive vinyl tiles. They tend to be thinner than other resilient products, the wear layer is usually on the skimpy side, and the choice of patterns and colors can be fairly limited. The adhesive is sticky, but it does not produce a "bed" for the tiles as troweled-on adhesive will, and as a result, self-adhesive tiles tend to curl up at the corners over time and generally require a fair amount of maintenance. If you choose to install them, it's always a good idea to purchase an extra carton of tiles so you can replace tiles that develop problems.

Self-adhesive vinyl tiles

The success of any tile-laying project depends on creating square layout lines and designing a pattern that is visually appealing and makes economical use of materials. For some basic pattern options, see the illustrations on pages 28 to 29.

1 Make certain a solid, flat and smooth layer of underlayment, usually ¼-in. plywood, is in place. Seams between sheets of underlayment and all screw heads in the underlayment should be covered with a smooth layer of floor leveler compound (See pages 20 to 25 for more information on installing underlayment). Vacuum the underlayment surface thoroughly. Apply a coat of underlayment primer **(See Photo A).** Primer creates a better bonding surface for the tile and is available wherever you purchase vinyl flooring. Follow manufacturer's application directions. Let the primer dry thoroughly.

2 Begin creating layout lines for the tile installation by determining the midpoint of the wall opposite the room entrance. At this midpoint, snap a chalkline across the floor, perpendicular to the wall **(See Photo B).** (See pages 30 to 31 for more information on establishing a perpendicular line.) Be careful not to track and embed grit onto the primed underlayment.

3 Measure and mark the midpoint of this line, and snap a perpendicular line through this point **(See Photo C).**

Diagonal patterns: For a diagonal tile layout, mark another reference line at a 45° angle to the perpendicular lines, through their point of intersection. You can use the 3-4-5 "right triangle" method for marking perpendicular lines for this, too— both angles opposite the right (90°) angle are 45° angles. After making

HOW TO INSTALL SELF-ADHESIVE VINYL TILES

PHOTO A Prepare the underlayment by filling all seams and screw head holes with floor leveler compound. Roll on a coat of underlayment primer to improve adhesion with the tiles.

PHOTO B Snap a reference line with a chalkline, approximately in the middle of the room. The line should be exactly perpendicular to the wall.

this diagonal reference line, mark a line perpendicular to it, again through the intersection of the first set of lines. Test the tile layout as shown below. Diagonal lines marked from corner to corner in a square room are usable reference lines—just make certain they are perpendicular to each other.

4 Leave the peel-off protective backing on the tiles and dry-lay a row of tiles along both lines to test the layout **(See Photo D).** A balanced layout has tiles of equal width and at least one half tile in size at the ends of a row. If an end tile will be narrower than one-half width, shift the row over so you won't have to cut and lay

PHOTO C Snap a second reference line exactly perpendicular to the first line. The line should extend all the way across the floor. If you are installing tiles in a diagonal pattern, snap reference lines that bisect the angles formed by the intersection of the first two reference lines.

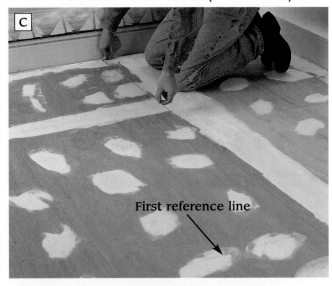

First reference line

PHOTO D Dry-lay tiles from the intersection point of the reference lines and toward each wall. In most cases, you'll need to cut the tiles at each end of the run: measure the distance from the last full tile to the wall at both ends of the dry-lay. For most pleasing visual results, the cut tiles should each be at least one-half their original size and they all should be the same size.

PHOTO E Adjust the layout as needed: in addition to the relative size of the end tiles, try to create a layout that centers either a seam or a tile in doorways. After the adjusted layout is set, snap chalklines that follow the edges of the tiles in each direction to create guidelines for laying the tiles. To avoid confusing these guidelines with the reference lines, use chalk of a different color.

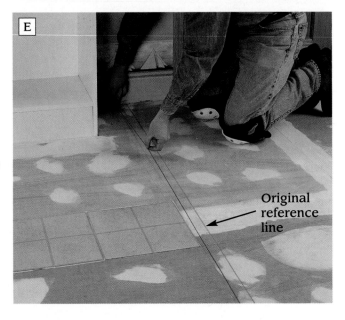

Original reference line

small pieces. Also, check where tiles end relative to outside corners and the room entrance. You want to avoid narrow tiles, and ideally a tile seam or a full width tile will fall at the exact center of the doorway. Hide any unbalanced layout area along a less visible wall, or behind appliances or other room elements, if possible.

5 Once you've adjusted the rows, snap new lines parallel to the original lines that mark the tile layout **(See Photo E).** Make certain these lines mark a seam between tiles, and cross out the original lines to prevent confusion when laying tile (or use a different color chalk). Check to be sure that the new lines are perpendicular to each other and adjust if necessary. Perpendicular lines are crucial for a quality installation.

6 Peel the protective backing from one tile and position the tile, aligning it in the corner of one quadrant of the layout **(See Photo F).** Prevent the adhesive back from sticking before the tile is in position by aligning only one tile edge along a line at the intersection of the layout lines, keeping the back of the tile off of the underlayment. Slowly lower the tile into place while keeping the edge in alignment. Press down firmly over the entire surface of the tile to bond the adhesive to the underlayment.

7 Prepare and position adjacent tiles along the layout lines in the quadrant on each side of the first tile **(See Photo G).** Keep the joints between tiles tight and take care not to overlap tile edges. If you misplace a tile, you should be able to pull it back up fairly easily, but do not reuse it. Discard it and use a fresh tile instead. Finish installing all the full-size tiles in the first quadrant.

8 Begin working on the next quadrant by installing tiles along the layout lines, then fill in

PHOTO F Once the adjusted layout lines are set, begin laying tile. Remove the backing and press the first tile so the edges align with both guidelines at their point of intersection.

the remaining full-size tiles. Fill in the full-size tiles in the remaining quadrants in similar fashion.

9 Since no adhesive is used when applying self-adhesive tiles, you're free to wait and install all non-full tiles after the uncut tiles are installed (this is generally the most efficient approach). See the tips on cutting holes (right) and cutting curves (next page). Cut all the tiles that need trimming and test the fit. Don't remove the backing until you're sure the tile piece fits its spot perfectly. Then remove the backing and install. To mark and trim square-cut tiles for the ends of rows, follow steps 10 and 11.

10 To fill in a partial tile along a wall or another straight edge, such as a base cabinet, position the tile to be trimmed face up directly over the last full tile in the row **(See Photo H).** Lay a ⅛-in.-thick spacer flat against the wall (this provides clearance for installing the tile). Place another full-size tile over the tile to be trimmed and slide it toward the wall until it butts against the spacer. Mark a line along the edge where the top tile overlaps the trimming tile. The visible portion of the trimming tile will be

PHOTO G Fill out the full tiles in the first working quadrant created by the guidelines, then apply tiles in the remaining quadrants, one at a time.

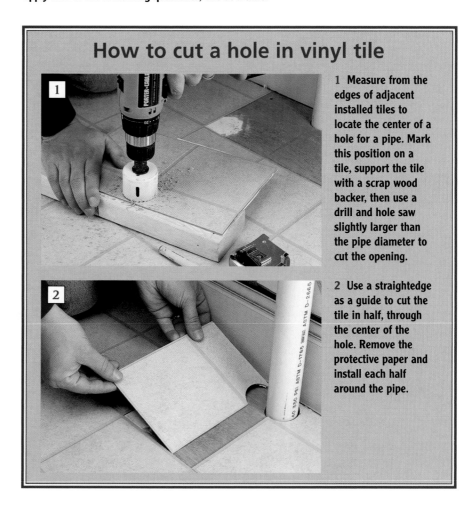

How to cut a hole in vinyl tile

1 Measure from the edges of adjacent installed tiles to locate the center of a hole for a pipe. Mark this position on a tile, support the tile with a scrap wood backer, then use a drill and hole saw slightly larger than the pipe diameter to cut the opening.

2 Use a straightedge as a guide to cut the tile in half, through the center of the hole. Remove the protective paper and install each half around the pipe.

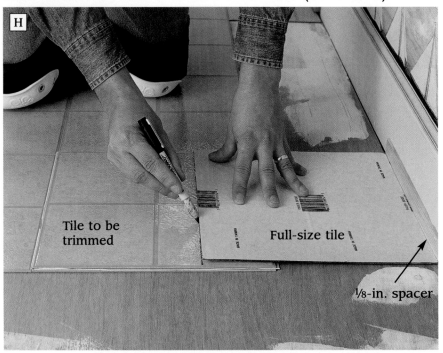

PHOTO H To mark tiles for trimming, lay the tile to be trimmed face-up on top of the last full tile in the row. With a spacer at the wall, lay another tile on top so it butts against the wall. Scribe a cutting line on top of the tile to be cut, following the edge of the top tile.

installed with the cut edge facing the wall. Use a straightedge guide and utility knife with a sharp blade to score the tile. Then, snap it in two at the scored line. Some resilient tile is thin enough that it can be cut completely through with one or two strokes of the knife. If the distance between a wall and the last row of full-size tiles varies no more than ⅜ in., it is more efficient to cut all the tiles at one time, rather than one at a time. Base molding will cover the gap. Use a jamb saw to cut door jambs so tile can be slipped underneath (See page 39).

11 Mark a notch in a tile as in step 10, marking the tile from both sides of the corner. After marking the tile from one side, position the tile over the full-size tile on the other side of the corner so the first marked line remains in the same position **(See Photo I).**

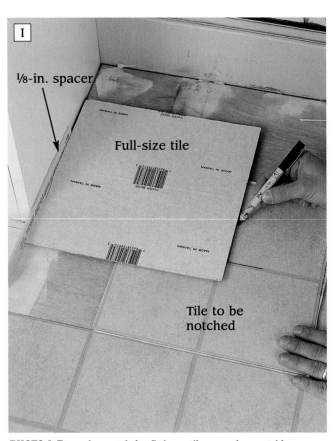

PHOTO I To mark a notch for fitting a tile around an outside corner or a base cabinet, simply use the method shown in PHOTO H to draw intersecting trim lines at one corner of the tile to be notched.

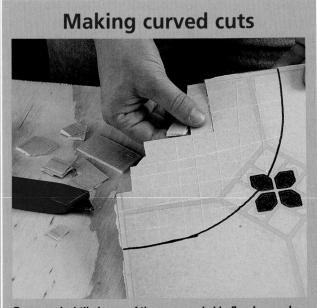

Making curved cuts

Because vinyl tile is one of the more workable flooring products, you can make fairly smooth curved cuts with little difficulty. The main risk when cutting curves is that the tile (especially thicker tiles) will tear or crease while you remove the waste. To prevent this, cut cross-hatches in the waste portion after scoring at least halfway through the tile along the cutting line. Remove the waste in sections, snapping it free along the cross-hatch cuts. If you're having difficulty getting the pieces to snap off cleanly (usually not a problem) try putting the tile in your freezer for 15 minutes first.

Cut the tile with a utility knife and straightedge guide. One leg of the cut can't be scored and snapped. If the tile is too thick to cut through with several strokes of a utility knife, use masking tape to temporarily attach the tile to scrap plywood and cut the notch with a jig saw.

12 When all the tiles are installed, roll the floor with a 100-pound flooring roller to make certain the adhesive is bonded to the underlayment **(See Photo J).** Avoid walking on the floor for at least 24 hours. Install thresholds in doorways and base molding (See page 58). For best results when cleaning, damp-mop the tiles with a vinyl tile detergent product.

PHOTO J Roll the tiled surface with a 100-pound flooring roller to create a more uniform floor that's well-bonded to the underlayment.

Repairing self-adhesive vinyl tiles

If a self-adhesive tile comes loose (a frequent problem) remove it by prying it up with a putty knife. If portions of the tile are still bonded to the underlayment, use a heat gun on low setting to soften the adhesive while prying the tile out. Be careful to direct the heat gun only at the damaged tile so surrounding tiles aren't loosened. After removing the tile, scrape the underlayment to remove any debris. Adhesive residue may require soaking with a water and detergent mixture before you can remove it with a scraper. Lightly sand the underlayment with fine sandpaper. Apply a coat of underlayment primer (See page 79) and let it dry. Remove the protective backing from a new piece of matching tile and install it. Press firmly over the entire surface of the tile to bond the adhesive to the underlayment. Place a flat weight over the entire tile for at least 24 hours.

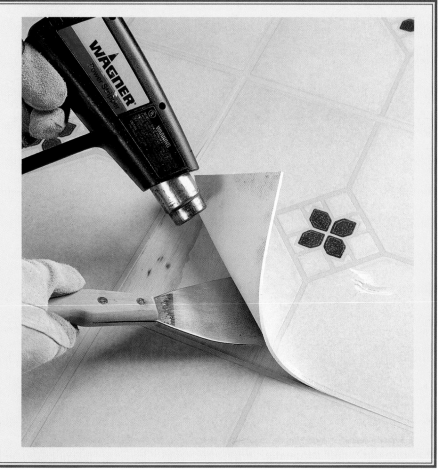

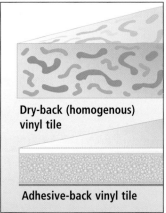

Dry-back vinyl tiles are installed in much the same manner as adhesive backed tiles, except that they are set into a bed of flooring adhesive that's troweled onto the floor underlayment.

Dry-back vinyl tiles

The two most common types of resilient vinyl tile you'll find in building centers are thinner, 12 × 12-in. adhesive-back tiles with traditional printed patterns (See previous chapter) and 12 × 12-in. homogenous dry-back vinyl tile (like the tile in the photo above). Both types cost about the same amount per square foot.

Dry-back (homogenous) vinyl tile

Adhesive-back vinyl tile

Dry-back vinyl tiles tend to be thicker and more durable than their adhesive-backed counterparts. You can purchase them with many of the same patterns commonly found on adhesive-backed tiles and sheet vinyl. Solid "homogenous" vinyl tiles with a commercial look (like the tiles shown above) are increasing in availability, even in general building centers, but you may need to go to a tile store to find them. Manufacturers now offer them in dozens of different colors with their distinctive "linoleum swirl."

HOW TO LAY DRY-BACK VINYL TILE

NOTE: The general layout information contained in the following sequence can easily be transferred to the installation of any type of floor tile, including ceramic tile.

1 Before starting your tile installation, prepare the floor underlayment as shown on pages 24 to 25. There are many ways of going about creating a layout for a tile flooring project. One of the most common is to base the layout on the primary entryway into the room. This area receives the most traffic and is the most visible. Remove or loosen transition pieces at adjoining floor coverings, then use a straightedge to draw a reference line at the entryway, parallel to the wall.

2 Mark the midpoint of the entryway area on the reference line (for example, if the door opening is 32 in. wide, measure 16 in. from one jamb). Since most vinyl tile is 12 in. square, the best layout is normally achieved by centering the middle tile on the midpoint, then trimming the end tiles in the opening to fit around the jambs. If you're installing smaller floor tiles, you may want the midpoint of the entry area to fall along a seam. For our 12-in. tiles, we measured over 6 in. from the midpoint and made a reference mark. Then we extended that reference mark out into the room with a framing square, making sure the line was perpendicular to the entryway.

First reference line

3 Establish perpendicular layout lines to divide the floor into quadrants. The first line is the extended reference line you drew in step 1. To locate the second reference line, dry-lay several tiles along the first line, starting with the first tile in the doorway (it should "underlap" the transition area). Then, trace the leading edge of the tile closest to the center of the room. With a framing square, extend this line in both directions from the first line. This will result in perpendicular lines that will fall at seam locations.

4 Begin applying tile adhesive for one quadrant of the layout. Until you're comfortable with the technique, apply adhesive for only a half-dozen tiles or so. Use a square-notched trowel to apply the adhesive (check the manufacturer's application recommendations before selecting a notched trowel). Coat the corner of the first quadrant using a square cross-hatch pattern of alternating ridge directions. Try not to obscure the layout lines.

5 Lay one corner tile in the quadrant, pressing it into the adhesive with a twisting motion. Take care not to displace too much of the adhesive, but make sure the tile is fully seated. The tile's edges should align with the layout lines in the corner.

6 Lay the tiles on each side of the corner tile, making sure they're flush against the edge of the corner tile and aligned with the layout lines. For our layout pattern, we alternated tile colors while we oriented the grain direction the same way for all tiles. Add the next tile in each run, then begin filling in the middle area. Apply tiles over the entire area that's coated with adhesive. Wipe up any squeeze-out at seams immediately.

7 Fill out the quadrant, taking care to maintain your tiling pattern. At the end (border) area of the quadrant, you'll probably need to cut tiles. To mark vinyl tiles for cutting, first slip a ¼-in. thick spacer next to the wall (do not run tiles flush up against the wall). Tile the field area up to the last row of full tiles, then lay a full tile (no adhesive) on top of the last tile row. Lay another tile on top of this one, but butt the end up against the spacer at the wall. Trace along the end farthest from the wall to mark a cutting line on the loose tile in the middle.

8 Cut the tiles for the border row with a utility knife and straightedge cutting guide. Lay the tile on a scrap wood backer board to avoid scarring the floor. For commercial resilient tiles (like those shown here) score the tile a couple of times along the cutting line, then snap it over the edge of a worksurface or board as you would when cutting wallboard. Thinner composition tiles should be cut all the way through with a utility knife. Install the cut tiles along the border.

9 Make cardboard templates for inside and outside corners, as well as for any obstructions you must tile around. Trace the template onto a tile and cut to fit.

10 Fill in the remaining quadrants. Avoid walking on freshly laid tiles. But if you must, lay down a piece of plywood scrap to distribute your weight.

11 When you're finished, make a final inspection of the seams to make sure there are no ridges between tiles. Then, roll the entire floor surface with a floor roller (a rental item). Let the tile dry undisturbed as long as required by the adhesive manufacturer.

12 Clean up any adhesive residue with a rag lightly dampened in mineral spirits, or another solvent if directed by the adhesive manufacturer. Install base trim (we used vinyl cove base adhesive). Because the commercial tile we installed does not have a glossy wear layer, we rented a floor buffer and applied three coats of floor wax for a high, protective gloss.

Sheet Vinyl

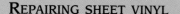

A seamless blanket of vinyl makes an excellent floorcovering choice for any bathroom, and can be effective in kitchens, basements and entryways as well. Most sheet vinyl sold at building centers is fairly neutral in color and pattern, which may not completely satisfy your design needs. But from a practical standpoint, it's hard to beat.

The introduction of resilient sheet flooring has created a minor revolution in bathroom and kitchen floorcoverings in the past generation. Among the many reasons for its popularity are the water-impervious, seamless surface it creates and its exceptionally low maintenance requirements when installed correctly.

There are two basic methods for installing resilient sheet flooring: *full-spread-bond,* where the entire sheet is glued to the floor underlayment with flooring adhesive; and *perimeter bond,* where only the border areas are bonded. For kitchens and bathroom, which tend to get quite a bit of traffic and are constantly exposed to moisture, a full-bond installation is recommended. Some manufacturers recently have developed resilient sheet flooring that is designed to be installed without adhesive bonding so it can be replaced easily as style trends change. Although it's a new and still somewhat unestablished product, you may want to ask your flooring distributor about it.

REPAIRING SHEET VINYL

1 Make a patch from a piece of the same sheet vinyl product (align the pattern) and lay it over the damaged area. Tape the edges down so it lies flat, then cut through both the patch and the flooring with a utility knife and straight-edge guide.

2 Remove the damaged section of sheet vinyl and scrape any residue from the underlayment with a putty knife. Spray the residue lightly with warm water and mild detergent to loosen it, if necessary.

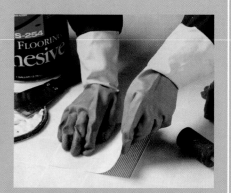

3 Apply flooring adhesive to the underlayment with a small notched trowel, then press the patch into the adhesive in the cutout area. Roll the patch with a J-roller, wallpaper seam roller or an old rolling pin. Wipe up adhesive squeeze-out with a damp rag.

HOW TO MAKE A FLOOR TEMPLATE

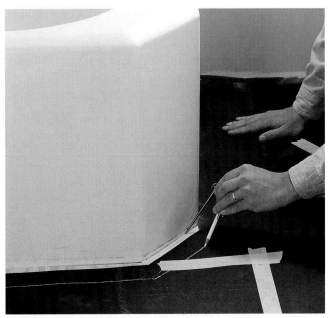

1 The surest way to guarantee a successful sheet flooring installation is to construct a full-size template of the room layout, including cutouts for obstructions like pipes and ductwork. You can use newspaper or kraft paper to make the template, but you'll get better results with 15# building paper or special-purpose template material sold by floorcovering manufacturers. Start by laying one piece of template material flat in a corner of the room, ¼ to ½ in. from each wall.

2 Tape additional pieces of template paper together in series, following the shape of the room. To keep the papers from sliding, make triangular cutouts in the paper, then tape the paper to the floor through the cutouts. Fill out as much of the field area as you can. Don't skimp with the masking tape: make sure the pieces are well-secured. When you reach obstructions or corners, cut smaller pieces of template material and trace the profile of the obstruction onto the material with a compass.

3 Cut out the template sheets and tape them in correct position relative to the wall. TIP: *Use a white colored pencil to draw cutting lines on building paper.*

4 Continue adding template material until the room-size template is completed. When using rigid material like building paper, it's not necessary to fill in the general field area in the center of the room, but if you're using flimsier material, make an entire "quilt" that's a mirror image of the floor area. Roll the template up loosely and transport it to the site (such as a garage) where you'll be cutting the flooring.

1 On a clean, dry, flat surface, lay the sheet vinyl pattern-side up, then fit the template (see previous page) on top of the sheet. Tape the template down to the sheet to prevent slippage. Take measurements to make sure the template is not distorted and check to make sure all of the cutout areas are the correct distance from the edges of the template. Transfer the pattern.

2 Slide the template out of the way, then cut the sheet vinyl along the cutting lines with a linoleum knife (be sure to slip a protective layer between the vinyl and the floor below). For round pipe cutouts, you can use a hole saw of the correct diameter for a clean cut. Intricate cuts can be made more easily with a pair of scissors than with a knife. Roll up the vinyl sheet.

3 Position the vinyl in the room and test the fit. Make any necessary adjustments, then fold or roll back half of the sheet. Apply flooring adhesive to the floor surface with a notched trowel, then set the vinyl into the adhesive.

4 Flip or roll the unbonded half of the sheet over the bonded half, apply adhesive to the floor, then set the second half. Be sure to get plenty of adhesive around cutouts for a good bond.

5 Roll the floor covering with a heavy floor roller (these can be rented at most building centers and rental centers), working away from the middle and toward the walls. Reinstall base shoe molding to cover gaps around perimeter.

How to make a seam in sheet vinyl

NOTE: The following information is for seaming sheet vinyl that is fully bonded to the floor.

1 Arrange the pieces to be seamed next to one another so the pattern (if any) aligns and repeats. The pieces should be exactly square to one another, with an overlap of 3 to 4 in. at the seam. Apply several pieces of heavy-duty tape (duct tape works well) across the seam to bind the pieces together. Dry-lay the sheet assembly in place and mark the location of the seam onto the floor. Remove the assembly and draw additional reference marks at the seam location. Apply flooring adhesive to the floor up to 12 in. from the seam location on one half of the area being covered by the sheets. Set the sheets into the adhesive with half of the sheet assembly folded back over the half being bonded. Then, apply adhesive to the other half of the area (to within 12 in. of the seam line) and lay the other half of the sheet assembly.

2 Roll the sheet assembly with a floor roller to set it into the adhesive. Then, lay a straightedge along the seam line and double-cut the two sheets with a utility knife held at an exact 90° angle to the floor surface.

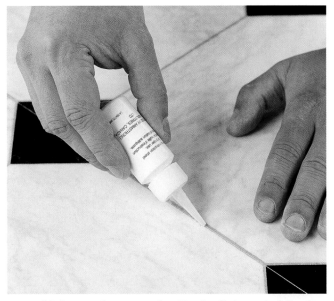

3 Fold back the edges of the sheets at the seam to expose the unbonded floor area. Apply adhesive to the area, then set the edges of the sheets into the adhesive. You may need to tug and push a little so the halves of the seam are exactly flush. Wipe up any adhesive that oozes up out of the seam, then roll each side of the seam with a floor roller or J-roller, rolling toward the seam to force any trapped air up through the gap. Let the adhesive set, then wipe the seamed area with a soft rag dipped in the solvent recommended by the manufacturer.

4 Weld the two sheets together. Nearly all sheet vinyl flooring installed in homes today is composed mostly of PVC, and can be solvent-welded in much the same way that PVC pipes are solvent-welded for plumbing. Some commercial tile can be heat-welded to close off the seam. The distributor that sold the sheet vinyl to you should also be able to provide a solvent-welding kit for seaming the flooring. The kit being used above (manufactured by Armstrong World Industries) consists of four separate chemical application steps. Follow the instructions and safety recommendations on your kit carefully.

Traditional padded carpeting offers a number of advantages over other floorcoverings, but ease of installation is not one of them. However, installing foam-backed carpet, as shown above, is a very manageable do-it-yourself project.

Carpeting

Carpet can be a relatively inexpensive floor covering in large rooms and over old flooring materials or subfloors with minor irregularities. It is softer, more comfortable flooring, particularly in bedrooms and family rooms. In cooler climate zones it provides warmer flooring than hard-surfaced materials such as tile and vinyl. This makes it ideal for family rooms and bedrooms and other areas that receive a great deal of traffic. However, carpet is not a good choice in bathrooms, kitchens or at entrances from the outside because it holds moisture and germs, stains easily and is more difficult to clean.

There are two basic types of carpet. Foam-backed carpet (also known as cushion-backed) has a polyurethane foam backing. It is generally less expensive and of lower quality than carpet installed over a separate pad. Foam-backed carpet is attached directly to the subfloor or old floorcovering with carpet adhesive or double-sided tape and is a simple do-it-yourself installation. This type of carpet also is easily replaced, making it great for kids' bedrooms and other family rooms that receive heavy wear and tear.

Conventional carpet is stretched over a separate underlayment pad and secured on tack strips. This requires special tools and techniques that are best left to professional installers, especially when carpeting large rooms. Most carpet suppliers provide a package deal combining the cost of carpet and installation that, when combined with the speed of professional installation, makes it difficult for the do-it-yourselfer to install carpet as quickly and inexpensively. This type of carpet is usually a higher-quality product and offers a greater range of colors, textures and styles than foam-backed carpet.

Carpet is available in five different kinds of fibers. *Nylon* is the most popular because it is very durable and cleans easily, but it is the most expensive of the synthetic fibers. *Olefin* (also known as polypropylene) is less expensive than nylon, and while not quite as durable, is very resistant to stains and fading. *Polyester* is the softest synthetic fiber but isn't very durable on its own and is often combined with nylon. *Acrylic* provides the feel and look of wool, but because it isn't very durable it is usually blended with other fibers. *Wool,* the only natural fiber used in carpet, is soft and wears well but is usually more expensive than synthetic carpet.

In addition to the the type of fiber, the cost of carpet is based on the density of the pile (the thickness of the fibers woven together). High-density pile costs more but wears better than low-density. Pile is generally *loop* (no loose fiber ends) or *cut* (fiber ends stand up like a brush), although some carpets combine both. Talk with a knowledgeable carpet supplier and get advice on the best carpet for your needs. Also, don't skimp on the pad for a carpet-and-pad installation. A quality pad should compress less than half its thickness when you pinch it between your fingers.

Cross-section of a carpet installation

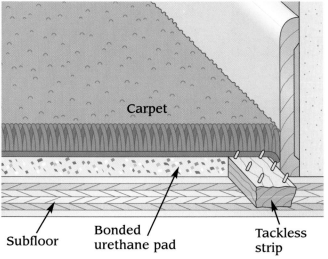

Subfloor / Bonded urethane pad / Tackless strip

A typical carpet installation is accomplished by tacking strips of wood with sharp metal points, called "tackless strips," around the perimeter of a room, then laying a pad on the floor, stretching carpeting over the pad and pressing the edges of the carpet between the tackless strips and the wall. The points in the tackless strip secure the carpeting. This type of installation is best left to professionals.

Carpet & pad types

Foam-back carpet (also called *cushion-back* or *kanga-back*) does not require a separate carpet pad and no stretching is needed for installation.

Conventional carpet doesn't have an attached pad backing. It is laid over a separate pad and stretched tightly onto the floor. It is by far the most common type.

Indoor/outdoor carpet is an unpadded, synthetic fiber material designed to be stapled or bonded directly to floors in wet areas.

Bonded urethane pad is often called "foam" pad and is the most common type of carpet pad.

Closed-cell foam pad resists deterioration and has a hard, slick surface coating for extra protection. It is more costly than other carpet pads.

Foam-back carpet

Conventional (unbacked) carpet

Indoor/outdoor carpet

Bonded urethane pad

Closed cell foam pad

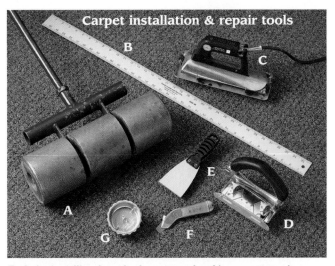

Carpet installation & repair tools

Tools for installing foam-back carpet and making carpet repairs include: 100-pound flooring roller (A); 3-foot straightedge (B); seaming iron (C); carpet edge trimmer (D); notched trowel (E); carpet knife with double-edged razor blades (F); carpet "doughnut" (G).

Foam-back carpet

PHOTO A Cut the carpet piece so it's about 1 ft. longer than each room dimension, then lay it out in the room, tugging and pulling to adjust it so the pattern and nap are straight and the carpet runs up each wall by 4 to 6 in.

Foam-back carpet is not everyone's first choice when it comes to carpeting, but if you want to install the carpet yourself it's the best product to use. It can be installed on just about any surface by bonding or tacking the edges to the floor.

With standard roll widths of 12 ft. (and sometimes 15 ft.), many rooms can be covered with one piece of carpeting. In square rooms with no significant obstructions, you can simply cut the carpet to length (and width if need be) then unroll it in the room and adjust it so it fits. If you need to use multiple pieces, install the first piece, then measure and cut additional pieces to fit. Try to orient the pieces so seams fall in low-traffic areas. Arrange the pieces so the seam is created by two factory edges—take this into account when cutting pieces to size, making sure the naps of the pieces are all running in the same direction. In non-square rooms, the most accurate way to measure and cut the carpet to fit is to create a full-size template from newspaper, as with sheet vinyl (See pages 89 to 90).

PHOTO B At corners, make a relief cut in the carpeting so it will lay flat on the floor against the wall. Be careful not to cut too far. Here, a carpeting knife is being used to make the relief cut in a corner.

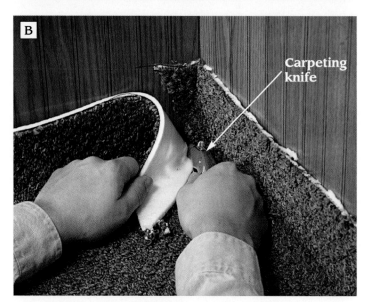

Carpeting knife

1 Lay the carpet piece in the room in rough position (if using multiple pieces, start with the largest one). Unroll and adjust the carpet so it laps up the walls relatively evenly—about 4 to 6 in. at each wall **(See Photo A).**

2 Make relief cuts at the corners so the carpet lies flat against the floor and against the walls **(See Photo B).**

PHOTO C Trim the carpet so it fits tight against the base of the wall. The best tool for this job is a carpet edge trimmer (these can be rented for little cost at most rental centers). The carpet trimmer forces the carpet against the wall as it trims, creating a cut that follows the wall exactly.

Carpet edge trimmer

3 Trim the carpet along the walls, using a carpet edge trimmer **(See Photo C).** Make certain to receive instructions for adjusting the edge trimmer to fit your carpet at the rental center. Be careful not to move the carpet out of alignment when making a cut.

4 Cut around obstacles, such as pipes or radiators, by folding the carpet up against the obstacle and making as short a cut to a carpet edge as possible **(See Photo D).** Position the cut carpet around the obstacle and trim the carpet to fit with a carpeting knife.

5 Once the carpet is cut to fit, weight down the carpet at one end of the room to keep it from slipping, then fold back half the carpet to expose the floor below.

6 Trowel a band of carpet adhesive about 1 ft. wide around the perimeter area of the exposed floor **(See Photo E).** (On a concrete floor or other smooth surface you can use double-sided carpet tape instead of adhesive.) Also apply adhesive under the seams cut to fit around obstacles.

7 Fold and roll the carpet back to its original position, taking care to avoid buckles and wrinkles. Press the carpet into the adhesive, then use a flooring roller to set it **(See Photo F).**

8 Move the weights, fold back the loose section of carpet and follow the same procedure to finish installing the carpet. If you need to create a seam between pieces, apply a wider band of adhesive in the seam area so both pieces will have an adhesive bed at least 1 ft. wide. When creating the seam, you'll likely need to tug and press a bit on the pieces to get them to fit together cleanly. Let the adhesive dry thoroughly before placing furniture in the room.

PHOTO D Cut around obstacles in the floor by slicing the carpet from the obstacle to the nearest wall, then making a cutout in the carpet that fits around the obstacle. When the carpet is bonded to the floor, the edges can be forced back together so the cut becomes invisible.

PHOTO E Fold back half of the carpet. Apply a band of carpet adhesive next to walls and obstacles you've trimmed around (in most cases, it's not necessary to fully bond the carpet to the floor). Use a trowel (size will be specified on the adhesive container) to apply the adhesive.

PHOTO F Roll back the folded carpet, setting the foam backing into the adhesive. Roll the bonded areas with a flooring roller, then fold the other half back over the bonded half. Apply flooring adhesive and install the second half of the piece.

Carpet Repair

Carpet brings an element of softness and warmth to a room, but it is also more easily damaged and more subject to wear than most other floorcoverings. Although there are limits to the amount and type of repairs you can perform on carpeting, an occasional quick fix can help you extend the life of your carpeting.

One of the most common places for carpeting to fail is along seams. Whether your carpet is bonded to the floor or stretched over a pad, try one of the quick-fix seam repairs shown on this page as soon you notice a seam has separated. Even if the repair isn't perfect, it will help prevent the separation form getting worse.

Minor damage, such as bad stains and cigarette burns, can be repaired by removing a small section of the carpeting and patching in with new material.

Repairing foam-back carpet seams

Repair foam-back carpet seams by carefully spreading carpet adhesive underneath the separated area, then forcing the seam together and weighting it down until the adhesive dries. Double-sided carpet tape also can be used if the floor underneath the seam is made of concrete or a similarly smooth surface.

HOW TO REPAIR A CARPET SEAM

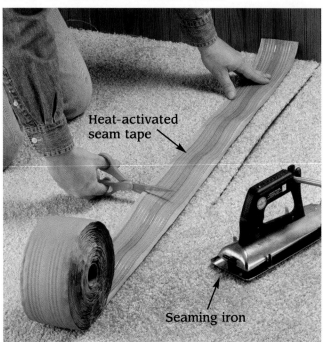

Heat-activated seam tape

Seaming iron

Work iron toward wall

Re-join unbacked carpet seams that have separated, using heat-activated carpet seam tape and a seaming iron, available at rental centers. Cut a piece of the tape several inches longer than the length of the separated seam (left photo). Place the tape glue-side up beneath the separated seam so it lies flat on the pad and extends past the seam on both ends. Insert the pre-heated seaming iron into the separated seam. Begin at one end and work toward the wall, slowly moving the seaming iron down the length of the tape to activate the glue. Force the carpet edges together tightly and flatten them into the hot glue as the iron moves down the seam (right photo). After using the seaming iron, press the seam area with weight for an hour to make certain it is bonded to the tape.

Carpet
doughnut

Patch

Damaged
carpet
(removed)

1 Make a circular cut to remove the damaged area, using a carpet knife and a round guide or a special carpeting tool called a "carpet doughnut," as shown above (it contains a razorblade in its rim and cuts a 3-in.-dia. circular hole). A circular patch is least likely to show. On foam-backed carpet, cut through the foam backing; cut through the carpet only and not through the pad on a carpet-and-pad installation.

2 Cut a patch out of identical carpet with the same method. If you don't have a remnant of the original carpet, cut the patch from carpet in an inconspicuous spot, such as in a closet or underneath a bed. Patch the inconspicuous area with carpet that resembles the original as closely as possible. Make sure the direction of the nap is the same on the patch as on the carpeting. Check the nap of the carpet pile by brushing your hand across the carpet. The pile will stand up when you brush against the nap and lie down with the nap.

3 Apply seam adhesive to the edge of the backing on the patch, then insert the patch into the hole.

4 Press down firmly to set the patch and surrounding carpet into the adhesive. Place a weight on the repair area for at least an hour.

options but should be covered with several coats of clear acrylic sealer or polyurethane to protect the finish. Porch-and-floor paint is either oil- or latex-based and has a hard, durable finish that will survive heavy use. The more limited range of colors and the high gloss and sheen of porch-and-floor paint may not be suitable for every interior floor. Masonry primer is applied to concrete floors before a finish coat of regular paint (follow primer manufacturer's directions which may include special floor preparation).

Painting a floor requires the same general painting tools and techniques used around the house. Remember, latex paint can be applied over oil-based primers and sealers, but oil-based paint should not be applied over latex. Use a short-nap sleeve when rolling, and make certain to use natural bristle brushes with oil-based paint and synthetic bristle brushes with latex paint. Don't forget your kneepads, since you will need to be on your hands and knees painting patterns or stenciling.

In addition to primer and paint, a few materials are necessary for a floor-painting project. *Wax stripper* removes the old wax floor finish. *Denatured alcohol* removes any remaining residue. *Floor leveler compound* or *wood putty* fill minor imperfections in flooring. *Acrylic sealer* or *polyurethane* seal raw wood prior to painting. *Painter's tape* and *stencils* are used to create a pattern.

TIPS:

• *Once you've applied primer, take off your shoes when working on the floor. It is easy to mar fresh, unprotected paint when laying out a pattern or applying another color coat.*

• *Apply a coat of stain-killing primer/shellac over knots in raw pine floors. This prevents the knots from bleeding through and staining the painted surface.*

Painting floors opens up a world of design possibilities at an economical price. Most wood, resilient and concrete floors can be painted with decorative treatments, like this stenciled border.

Painting Floors

Paint presents many wonderful creative options for a floor, with infinite possibilities for customized design. Almost any decorative painting technique can be used on a floor, from colorwashing and faux finishes to stenciling. You also can use paint to provide a striking

new flooring surface on existing wood, concrete, sheet vinyl, linoleum and some flooring tiles. This is particularly useful when the existing flooring has gone out of style, shows wear or has minor imperfections but otherwise has plenty of life left.

Three types of paint can be used on a floor. Regular oil-based or latex paint offers the most design

Repeating geometric patterns have a dramatic effect and are easy to paint. For best results, use masking tape to lay out the pattern, or use a painting template.

Contrasting borders add visual interest to a floor, giving the room a sense of completeness. But be aware that a painted border treatment will tend to make small rooms appear even smaller.

Trompe l'oeil is the technique of using paint to trick the eye into thinking it sees objects that aren't really there. In its simplest form, it can be used to create "faux" finishes that resemble brick pavers, genuine wood grain or even Oriental carpet patterns.

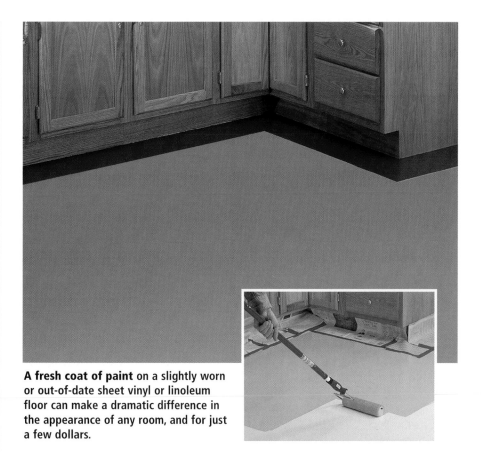

A fresh coat of paint on a slightly worn or out-of-date sheet vinyl or linoleum floor can make a dramatic difference in the appearance of any room, and for just a few dollars.

Concrete floor finishes

Sealer   Stain   Paint   Epoxy

Painting & treating concrete floors

There are several finishes you can apply to make a concrete floor more attractive and easier to clean. *Concrete sealer* is a clear product that helps the concrete resist staining and creates a "slick" surface that's easier to sweep but isn't slippery; *concrete stain* is essentially sealer with a coloring agent for visual appeal; *concrete paint* seals and beautifies the floor, but because the product has more body it will fill small voids and cracks, eliminating areas where dirt, mildew and even insects can collect; *epoxy paint* is a two-part finish that prevents moisture seepage up through the floor, resists stains and spills and has a very attractive appearance.

Preparing Floors for Painting

As is true with all painting, preparation is the key to successful floor painting. The floor should be clean, dry and stable. If the flooring is waxed, remove the wax with a wax stripper (paint will not adhere to wax), then clean the flooring with denatured alcohol. Any damaged areas should be repaired and primed before further work.

Existing flooring materials and old finishes on wood floors should be sanded lightly to provide a better bonding surface for new paint. If the finish on a wood floor is peeling or otherwise failing, strip it completely by sanding to raw wood (see pages 66 to 71 for more information on

sanding a wood floor). Don't use chemical strippers to remove old finishes before painting. They may leave chemical residue on the flooring, which may react with chemicals in the paint and cause the paint finish to fail.

Paint will not fill in imperfections in the flooring. Small holes and other minor damage should be repaired. Any repairs you make must be sanded and feathered into the surrounding flooring if you want to produce a smooth painted surface. Flooring needing many repairs should be replaced rather than painted—it is difficult to achieve a quality finish on a floor full of patches.

TIPS FOR FLOOR PREPARATION

Scrape off any old adhesives, backings or other residue from the floor surface with a sharp floor scraper.

Use a random-orbit sander to remove ridges left by old paint or other surface imperfections. Depending on your objective, you can often get by with simply feathering the ridges out so hard lines are knocked down (but any remaining old paint must be solidly bonded to the floor).

Fill cracks, holes and deep splinters with floor leveler compound or wood putty. Start by cleaning out the defect (remove any wood or other material that is splintered or at all loose), then fill the hole with compound (left photo). Overfill the area slightly. Once the compound or putty had dried thoroughly, sand it down so the surface is level with the surrounding floor surface (right photo).

Thoroughly scrub the floor with hot water and detergent to remove dirt and wax build-up. If your existing floor covering has more than a handful of dime-sized or bigger damaged areas, it is not a good candidate for painting. Floors with a glossy finish should be scuff-sanded with 100-grit sandpaper, then vacuumed.

A floor polisher with a fine-mesh screen is an excellent tool for sanding or scuffing old flooring materials in preparation for new paint. It covers a large floor area quickly and is much easier on the knees and back than any other method. Clean the floor thoroughly after sanding or scuffing. Make sure to use a screen and not a steel pad; any metal fibers left on the floor may rust and stain your work.

Remove old floor wax before painting a floor. If any wax is present the paint will not bond correctly to the floorcovering and the paint job will fail quickly. Specially formulated floor stripping products are very effective for this task (left photo). Be sure to read and follow the manufacturer's application instructions carefully, making sure to wear protective rubber gloves and provide adequate ventilation. Once the old wax is removed, wash the floor surface with denatured alcohol to dissolve any remaining residue (right photo).

How to paint a floor

1 Prepare the floor as directed on the previous two pages. Apply a coat of primer (use masonry primer on concrete floors) with a roller and extension handle **(See Photo A).** Use a paint brush to cut in edges and around obstacles. Tint the primer in the range of the finish coat, or the lightest color of a multiple-color pattern. Begin painting in a corner opposite a room entrance and work back toward the doorway. Let the primer dry thoroughly.

2 Lay out any pattern planned for your painted floor, including stencils. Use painter's masking tape and press the edges to make certain paint won't bleed under it **(See Photo B).** Measure and mark perpendicular reference lines as guides for the tape for borders or other patterns requiring them.

3 Apply the first coat of final color, using a brush or roller as necessary **(See Photo C).** Apply one or two more coats. When the last coat is dry, pull up the masking tape and lay out new tape for the next color. Continue this process until the pattern is complete. When the final coats are dry and the tape is removed, apply two or three thin coats of non-yellowing polyurethane over the floor to protect the paint. Use either oil-based or water-based polyurethane.

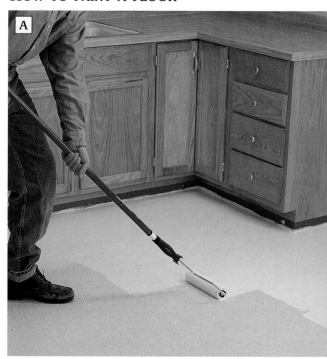

PHOTO A Apply a primer that's tinted to match the same general tone as the dominant color to be used. If you're applying contrasting color, the primer should match the lightest color tone. You can use either oil-based or latex primer (if painting concrete, use masonry primer).

PHOTO B Lay out your pattern, if you're using multiple colors. We used masking tape to mark off an 8 in. wide border around the perimeter of the room. For borders, checkerboard and other geometric patterns, measure and draw reference lines for the masking tape.

PHOTO C We applied two coats of red paint at the border, then removed the tape, masked off the border area, and rolled two coats of moss-colored paint into the field area. Make sure to allow plenty of time for the paint to dry between coats. After all the paint has dried fully, apply wo or three coats of glossy, non-yellowing polyurethane (either latex or oil-based). For a photo of the finished floor, see page 99.

Stenciling

Stencils can be used to add interest and individuality to a painted (or even an unpainted) floor. Most commonly used as border treatments, stencils may also be applied in an all-over fashion or to emulate the look of an expensive carpet.

Stenciling, when done patiently, is almost foolproof. You can stencil a simple, one-color design or choose a more complex pattern with multiple colors. Whether it's paint, raw wood, vinyl or even unglazed ceramic tile, it's important that the base be properly prepared to accept paint before you start (See pages 100 to 101).

When stenciling a pattern on a floor, you'll need some type of reference line. In the project shown here, we applied stencils along a painted border and used the border for reference; in other cases, you'll want to snap a chalkline or two for reference (use blue chalk—red is much harder to remove).

The best paints for stenciling are thicker, fast-drying types that are less likely to run under the stencil.

Stencil options

Make your own. Most craft stores sell durable plastic stenciling blanks. Simply trace the pattern you want to stencil onto the blanks, then carefully cut out the areas to receive paint with a razor knife. If you're using multiple colors, trace around the cutouts with markers indicating the correct color.

Purchase stencils. Craft stores and many building and decorating centers sell a wide variety of pre-fashioned stencils suitable for floors and walls. Many of these also come with helpful instructions and hints for applying the pattern.

How to Stencil a Floor

1 After the base coat of paint (if any) is dry, tape your stencil to the floor securely. Especially if you're using a pattern with a regular repeat, begin with the center of the stencil in the midpoint of the room or stencil area (this ensures that your pattern will end at the same point at both ends of the room).

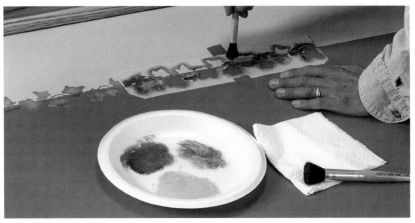

2 Mix the stenciling paint on a paper or foam plate, then dab a stenciling brush (also called a stippling brush) into the paint, blending the colors if you choose. Use a separate brush for each color. Move the brush lightly in a circular motion until the bristles are loaded. Apply the paint in a straight downward, pecking motion (called stippling). After the stencils are filled in, carefully remove the stencil. Reposition the dry stencil to continue your pattern. When you're finished, apply two or three coats of topcoat (such as polyurethane) to the entire floor (See pages 69 to 71).

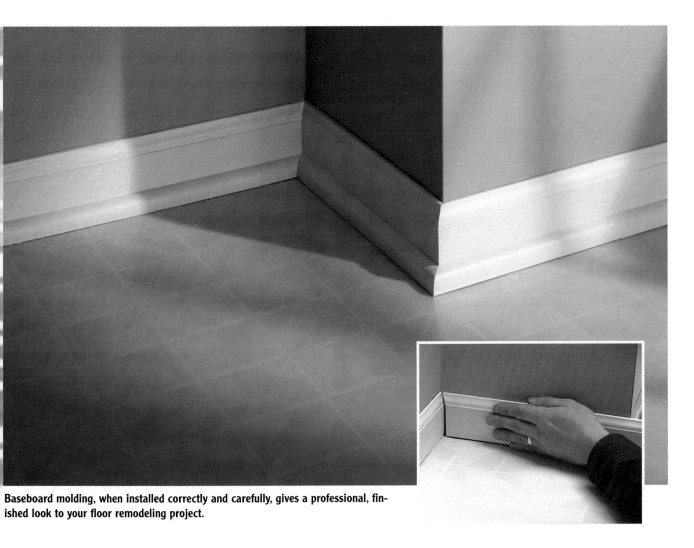

Baseboard molding, when installed correctly and carefully, gives a professional, finished look to your floor remodeling project.

Baseboard

Most floor projects are not complete until the installation of baseboard molding. This step of the floor remodeling process not only creates an attractive transition between floor and walls, it also has a more practical purpose: to cover expansion gaps or the rough edges of flooring at the room's perimeter. Installing baseboard moldings is a relatively simple project, although some fairly precise work is required.

Installing baseboard

When installing baseboard, determine an installation sequence with as few mitered or coped joints as possible. Baseboard on the wall opposite the room entrance should have butt joints at both ends—the coped joints of the adjoining pieces won't be as noticeable if wood movement causes them to open up. The best installations have one continuous piece of molding on each length of wall, but you can splice two pieces together on a long wall with a *scarf joint.* You will have a much easier installation when as many

molding pieces as possible have a butt joint on at least one end. That way, the coped or mitered joint can be cut and fitted before trimming the piece to length. Even if the piece ends up a little short because of extra cuts, the coped joint of the adjoining piece will cover the butt joint on the short end. If possible, avoid terminating the installation sequence with a molding piece that requires mitered or coped joints on both ends. Making tight mitered or coped joints at both ends without cutting the piece too short can be difficult.

Once you've established a plan, calculate how many lineal feet of molding you'll need by combining the measurements of shorter pieces that can be cut out of the stock lengths available at the building center (usually between 8 and 14 ft. long). Purchase about 10% extra to allow for waste.

If you plan on painting the baseboard, prime both sides, but cut and install it before you apply the finish coat of paint. Fill nail holes with putty and plug any gaps at joints with caulk (caulk is better than putty because it can flex as the wood moves). After the prep work is done, then apply the paint. If staining the baseboard, stain both sides of molding before installation. Fill nail holes and gaps with color-matched putty.

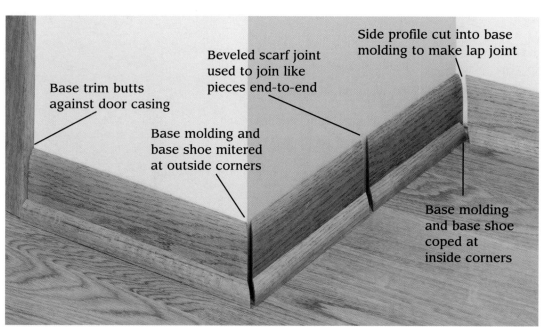

Base trim butts against door casing

Beveled scarf joint used to join like pieces end-to-end

Side profile cut into base molding to make lap joint

Base molding and base shoe mitered at outside corners

Base molding and base shoe coped at inside corners

Baseboard molding is required on every wall to cover the gap between the floor and the wall. It can be as simple as plain ranch molding, or you can dress it up a bit by combining different molding styles (See below). Most joints are miter-cut at a 45° angle. In some cases, you'll need to cut the side profile of one adjoining piece so it fits around and against the other, as in the inside corner shown above.

Pine   Phillipine mahogany   Oak   Artificial

Common wood types used for moldings include oak, Phillipine mahogany and pine. Recently, manufacturers introduced paintable moldings made from reconstituted wood and other products. While inexpensive and suitable for some applications, artificial moldings are not as durable as genuine wood products. TIP: *When trying to match wood tones with the rest of the trim in your home, dab a little water on the molding sample. The wet color will be close to the actual color when a clear topcoat is applied.*

Bevel your base shoe

For a more finished appearance, bevel the exposed ends of base shoe molding at about a 45° angle.

MOLDING COMBINATIONS FOR CREATING BASE TRIM

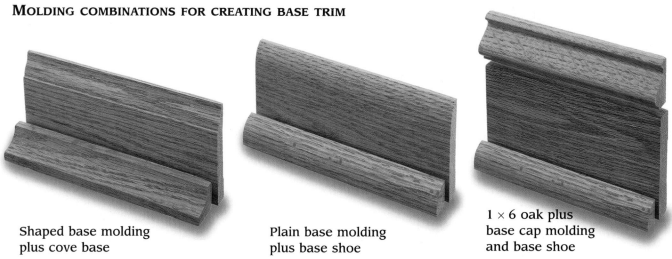

Shaped base molding plus cove base

Plain base molding plus base shoe

1 × 6 oak plus base cap molding and base shoe

1 Use a tape measure and chalk-line to mark a level line on the walls around the perimeter of the room for alignment of the top of the baseboard molding **(See Photo A).** Floors that aren't perfectly level are common—make certain that the distance between the line and the floor is equal to the height of the baseboard at the narrowest point in the room, adjusting the line if necessary.

2 Begin the installation on the wall opposite the main entrance into the room. This piece of baseboard should have a square butt joint at each end. Measure the length needed, then cut the piece ¹⁄₁₆ in. longer than necessary, using a miter saw. Bevel the cuts very sightly so the board is a bit longer at the back than in front (called *back cutting).*

3 Position the baseboard, bowing out the center slightly, so both ends butt squarely against the adjacent walls **(See Photo B).** Release the molding and it will snap into place, the back-cut ends digging into the walls. Drive and set nails at every wall stud, about 1 in. from the top of the molding, and into the sill plate.

4 Rough-cut the next piece so it's about 4 in. longer than needed to allow for fitting the coped end. Cut a 45° miter in the end that will adjoin the butt-jointed end of the first piece of molding **(See Photo C).** Make this cut so the backside of the molding is longer than the front face.

5 Use a coping saw to cut along the exposed profile of the front face created by the miter **(See Photo D).** This is called "coping" the joint. Hold the saw so it makes a back cut at about a 60° angle.

6 Place the coped end over the adjacent baseboard to test-fit the joint **(See Photo E).** Make any adjustments with a wood rasp or

PHOTO A Snap a chalkline to mark a level reference line on the walls around the perimeter of the room for alignment of the top of the baseboard molding.

PHOTO B Position the baseboard, bowing out the center slightly, so both ends butt squarely against the adjacent walls. Release the molding and it will snap into place.

sharp utility knife. Once the coped joint fits well, cut the piece to final length, leaving it ¹⁄₁₆ in. long. Position and nail the molding piece as in Step 3. Continue installing molding pieces around the room.

7 To cut miters for the outside corner, first use a scrap of molding to mark the molding position on the floor at both sides of the corner, making certain to mark the spot where pieces will intersect on the floor **(See Photo F).**

8 Rough-cut a piece of baseboard for one side of the corner, about 4 in. longer than needed. Position the piece against the wall and mark where the piece crosses the wall corner and where it

crosses the intersection marked on the floor **(See Photo G).**

9 Place the molding piece on the miter saw and make a test cut about 2 in. from the marks. Cut this miter so the back is shorter than the front **(See Photo H).** Don't attach this piece yet.

10 Follow the same procedure for the molding piece on the other side of the corner. When both final miters are cut, test fit the joint. Make small adjustments with a wood rasp or sharp knife. If the edge of one piece is slightly proud of the other, it is best to bring it flush with a file or sandpaper, rather than re-cutting. If the walls aren't square, you may need

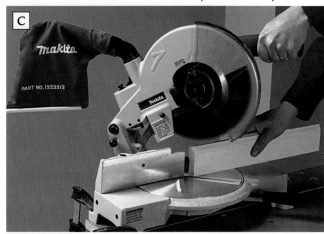

PHOTO C Rough-cut the next piece so it's about 4 in. longer than needed, then cut a 45° miter in the end that will adjoin the butt-jointed end of the first piece of molding.

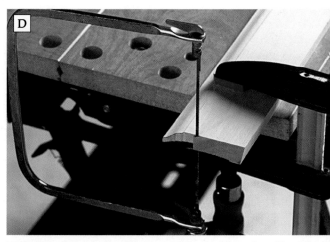

PHOTO D Use a coping saw to cut along the exposed profile of the front face created by the miter. Experiment to determine the best coping saw angle; depending on the profile, some portions of the profile may require cutting at a different angle than others.

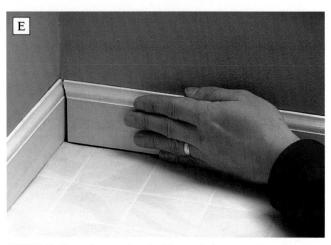

PHOTO E Place the coped end of the workpiece over the adjacent baseboard to test-fit the joint. Once the coped joint fits well, cut the piece to final length, leaving it 1/16 in. long.

PHOTO F To cut miters for the outside corner, use a piece of molding to mark the position of the front edge of the molding on the floor at both sides of the corner.

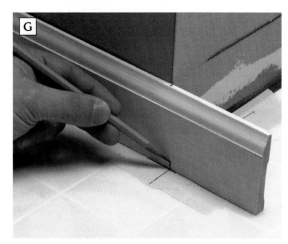

PHOTO G Position the molding piece for one side of the corner against the wall and mark where the piece crosses the wall corner and where it crosses the intersection marked on the floor.

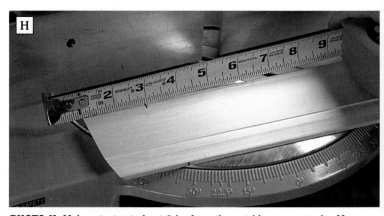

PHOTO H Make a test cut about 2 in. from the outside corner marks. Measure between the cut and the marks. If the distance is equal, make a final cut at the marks. If the distance isn't equal, adjust the molding position on the saw table—either raising slightly the front end or the back end of the molding piece—and make another cut. Continue making adjustments as necessary until you can make the final cut. Do not attach this piece yet.

PHOTO I Cut the second outside corner piece the same way as the first. When both final miters are cut, test fit the joint. If the walls aren't square, you may need to shim under the molding before cutting to bring the miters into alignment.

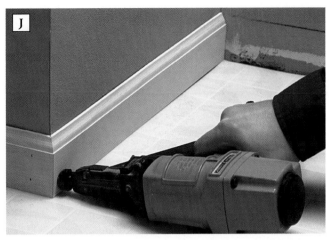

PHOTO J Attach the corner pieces. We used a pneumatic nail gun—an unbeatable tool for installing trim. A hammer, combined with a nailset, will also get the job done.

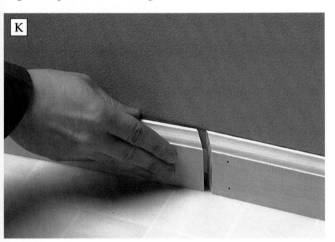

PHOTO K If you need to join two boards in mid-run, cut a 45° scarf joint to create a tight, inconspicuous seam.

PHOTO L Attach base shoe or quarter round molding after the baseboard is installed.

to shim under the molding before making the final cut **(See Photo I).** Once your miter joint fits together tightly, cut the other end of each board to get the workpiece to correct length. Nail to the wall **(See Photo J).**

11 If two pieces of molding must be spliced together, make a *scarf joint* with 45° miters **(See Photo K).** Position the pieces on the wall and test-fit the joint. Make adjustments with a wood rasp or sharp knife. When the joint fits well, attach the molding piece that forms the bottom of the scarf joint first, then attach the mating piece.

12 Continue installing the baseboard pieces. See the Tips to the right for information on dealing with various cutting situations. Install base shoe molding (See page 106). Make sure all nailheads are set, fill holes with putty and touch up the finish if needed.

Cutting Tips:

- *If a molding piece must have a mitered end and a coped end, cut the cope joint first. On a piece with miters at both ends, first fit the joints on all of the pieces it contacts before attaching any of the pieces. This allows for minor adjustments.*

- *The length of a molding piece with coped joints at both ends is the distance between the profile edges. But rough cut the piece longer to allow for the miters that expose the coping profiles.*

- *Where baseboard is thicker than the door jambs or vent covers it butts against, use a power miter saw to cut a bevel on the corner of the baseboard to make a more attractive transition (See Tip, page 106).*

CEILING PROJECTS

Ceiling Remodeling Projects

**Wallboard Ceilings
(Pages 114 to 122)**

**Texturizing Ceilings
(Pages 123 to 127)**

**Suspended Ceilings
(Pages 136 to 143)**

**Metal Panel Ceilings
(Pages 144 to 149)**

Ceiling Projects

There is a wealth of materials and methods available for turning a plain ceiling into a striking feature of a room's decor.

The choice between a smooth or textured ceiling finish will determine the kind of work done to the ceiling surface. Smooth finishes are created with paint or wallpaper. Textured finishes can be made with wallpaper, texturing products sprayed onto the ceiling surface or by adding a new surface of pressed metal panels. If access to electrical, plumbing or heating and cooling systems is necessary, then choose a suspended ceiling.

Evaluate the condition of the existing ceiling. A smooth surface requires a flat ceiling without noticeable blemishes. Minor repairs of cracks, small holes or water stains may be all that's needed to make the ceiling surface ready. But uneven joists or major repairs will show through. This means the old ceiling should be replaced. New wallboard should be installed with smooth joints for a blemish-free surface.

Ceiling moldings are an exceptional finishing touch for many rooms. Their installation requires trim carpentry skills and patience.

Prepare for a ceiling project like you would for any remodeling project. Wear appropriate eye, ear and respiratory protection. Cover doorways and duct work openings with plastic. Check with the local building inspector for any code regulations affecting your project, and make certain inspections for electrical and plumbing work, if necessary, are completed before installing new wallboard. Remember that electrical boxes that contain live cables can't be covered with wallboard or other materials (a solid box coverplate is necessary so the wires can be accessed). Empty or disconnected electrical boxes may be covered.

Removing old ceiling surfaces

Removing plaster and lath: Protect flooring with a layer of thick cardboard covered with a tarp. Wear safety glasses and a dust mask. Pull down any loose areas. Use a maul or the flat side of a hammer against the plaster surface between joists to break it loose from the keys holding it to the lath. Then slip a pry bar behind the plaster to finish pulling it off the ceiling. Work carefully around electrical boxes since they may be attached to the plaster. Make certain the power is off to the boxes. Work in small sections and not directly overhead as plaster is surprisingly heavy. Force the pry bar behind the lath at the joists to pry it off. Remove any nails in the joists that don't come off with the lath. Wallboard can be installed over lath, but if wiring or plumbing work is necessary, remove the lath.

Removing wallboard: Protect flooring as for a plaster ceiling and wear safety glasses and a dust mask. Snap chalklines between joist locations and cut along the lines. Make certain you know the location of any electrical and plumbing in the ceiling and that the power is off to fixture boxes. Cut just deeply enough to sever the wallboard. A wallboard saw takes more effort but is neater. A circular saw is quick but messy. Break and pull the wallboard away from the joists. A pry bar will be helpful. If screws attach the wallboard, use a drill/driver to remove them.

ROCK® Brand
Gypsum Panel
Tapered Edge
FIRECODE® CORE
FIRECODE® CORE
SHEETROCK® Brand
Gypsum Panel
Tapered Edge
SHEETROC
USG
USG

Installing Wallboard Ceilings

Creating a beautiful ceiling surface where there was once old cracked plaster is just one of the benefits offered by this basic and versatile project. Install a new wallboard ceiling in additions and other new construction building projects. Wallboard installation techniques also are used when making ceiling repairs.

Install ½-in.-thick wallboard on ceiling joists that are spaced 16 in. on-center. Trusses spaced 24 in. on-center require ⅝-in.-thick wallboard. Some building codes require ⅝-in.-thick wallboard on all ceilings; check with your local building inspector for requirements concerning your project. If you are covering over an existing ceiling surface (of cracked plaster, for example) ½-in. or even ⅜-in. material is fine, but make certain you use screws long enough to penetrate into the ceiling joists at least 1 in. When installing wallboard in a bathroom ceiling above a shower or another wet area, use water-resistant wallboard (which usually has a green paper surface and is often called "greenboard").

Prepare for your wallboard project by sealing the project area from the rest of your house: wallboard dust is very fine and penetrates nearby areas easily. Cover doorways, heating/cooling vents and other large openings with plastic sheeting. Tarps laid over a layer of cardboard will protect flooring. Spread a tarp outside the room entrance to prevent tracking wallboard dust into other rooms. Remember to wear eye and respiratory protection when working with wallboard, as the dust is an irritant.

Make sure ceiling joists are straight and spaced properly. Use cross blocking between joists to straighten curved joists and add 2 × 4 nailers when joists are spaced too far apart. See the Tip on page 129 for information on leveling uneven ceiling framing. Also, make certain there are adequate nailing surfaces for attaching the wallboard. No edge of a sheet should be unsupported for more than 2 ft. Extra nailing surfaces often are needed at non-load-bearing walls and on vaulted ceilings.

Wallboard T-squares are used to square and measure sheets of wallboard for cutting, and can be used as cutting guides.

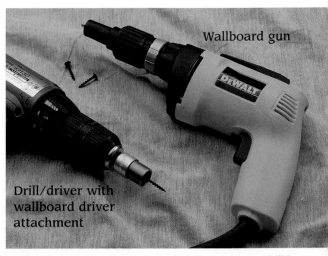

Wallboard guns and special attachments for your power drill keep you from overdriving wallboard screws.

Wallboard knives come in a variety of blade widths for spreading joint compound. Wallboard hawks are hand-held metal trays that make handling smaller quantities of joint compound easier.

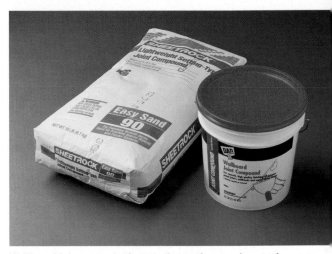

Wallboard joint compound comes in two forms—dry powder or premixed in one- or five-gallon pails. Premixed is more convenient, but the dry-mix is cheaper and tends to shrink less.

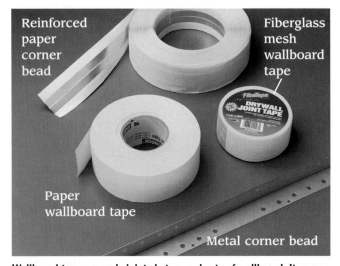

Wallboard tape conceals joints between sheets of wallboard. It comes in paper or fiberglass mesh forms. Corner bead is used to create inside or outside corners.

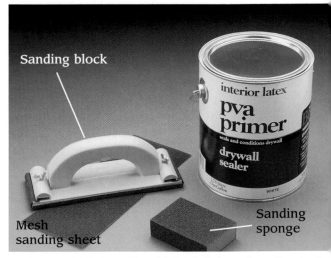

Finishing materials for wallboard joints include mesh sanding sheets and a sanding block, a sanding sponge for final sanding and wallboard sealant to apply before painting.

Wallboard Ceilings

Before installing wallboard on the ceiling, make certain inspections for plumbing, electrical and insulation have been completed. If your project includes insulation and the insulation is unfaced, install a proper vapor barrier before attaching the wallboard. Make certain a metal protector plate covers any spot where wiring or pipes are closer than 1½ in. to the edge of the joist.

Install wallboard sheets perpendicular to the ceiling joists, and stagger the end seams. This provides the greatest ceiling strength and will help prevent cracks or sagging seams. Determine a layout that uses the fewest pieces, for economy and ease of installation. Use the following method to estimate the number of sheets needed:

How to estimate wallboard materials:
- Divide the square footage of the ceiling (length times width) by 32 (the square footage of one 4 × 8-ft. sheet)
- Add 10% for waste, then round up to the next full sheet (a multiple of 32). You usually can return unused sheets.
- For every 1000 square feet of wallboard, purchase 370 ft. of paper tape, 140 pounds of premixed joint compound and 700 screws.

Always cut wallboard through the finish surface and install the wallboard so the finish surface faces the room. The finish surface is smoother and a lighter color than the back (usually a darker gray). Change blades frequently in your utility knife. Sharp blades make accurate cuts much more easily, but the dense wallboard material quickly dulls the blades.

Use wallboard screws when attaching the wallboard to the ceiling joists. Screws make a more stable ceiling and there is much less risk of "pops" than with nails. Use nails to quickly tack a sheet into position when it is more awkward to use a screw gun, but finish attaching the sheet with screws. Use screws long enough to penetrate at least 1 in. into the ceiling joists.

The cutting and installation techniques shown here will help you do quick and accurate work. It may take a few cuts to get the feel of the tools and how the techniques work, but you will soon find yourself working just like a professional.

1 Snap a chalkline perpendicular to the joists 4 ft. (the width of a full sheet) out from the starting wall. Establishing a perpendicular first row of sheets will make installing the remaining rows much easier.

2 Start the first row of wallboard with as long a sheet as possible. Measure from the side wall to the center of a joist for the length you need. The distance from the wall to the center of the last full joist 96 in. away or closer will be the length of the first sheet you install. Cut the wallboard sheet to length by scoring along the face with a utility knife, using a straightedge (such as a wallboard T-square) as a guide. Score deeply, then snap the sheet along the scored line. Cut through the backing at the break.

3 Set the sheet on the wallboard lift with the back side facing the ceiling joists and raise it into position (wallboard lifts can be rented at most rental centers). Make certain the sheet is properly aligned with both walls in the corner, or to the perpendicular line, and the end is centered on the joist.

4 Drive wallboard screws every 8 in. at edges and every 12 in. in the field (at joist locations). Keep screws at least ³⁄₈ in. back from an edge so they don't break the edge. Drive each screw until it sets below the face of the wallboard, but not far enough to tear the paper surface (see inset photo). A screw gun has an adjustable depth setting for this. You can buy depth-setting attachments for regular drills. Install a full sheet at the end of the first sheet, leaving a ¹⁄₁₆-in. gap at the butt joint. This gap allows joint compound to penetrate and strengthen the seam.

5 Measure from walls or the edge of an adjacent installed piece to position notches or holes that need to be cut. Measure to both sides of an electrical ceiling box or recessed light can to get the proper position. Remember to allow for the ¹⁄₁₆-in. gap between wallboard sheets.

Wallboard Jack

A homemade alternative to renting a wallboard lifter (See step 3) is the wallboard jack, a handy lifting device made of 2 × 4s. The jack should be an inch or two taller than the distance from the wall to the bottoms of the joists.

6 Use a compass to scribe circular cutouts. Trace the outline of an electrical box of the same dimensions for box cutouts. Cut outside the lines to make certain there is enough clearance. Use a keyhole saw or specialty wallboard saw to make the plunge cut for an electrical box or recessed light cutout. The keyhole saw cuts curves easily.

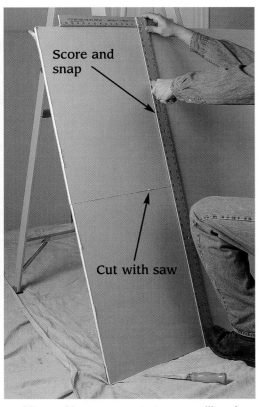

Score and
snap

Cut with saw

7 After marking a corner cutout, use a wallboard saw to cut the shorter leg of the corner. Then score and snap the remaining leg.

8 Continue installing full sheets in a similar manner to finish the row, trimming the last sheet to length if necessary. Install the remaining rows the same way, cutting notches and holes as necessary. Remember that the end seams should be staggered. Often this can be accomplished by beginning the next row at the side of the room at which the previous row ended. Make certain to leave a 1/16 in. gap between the tapered edges of adjacent wallboard sheets.

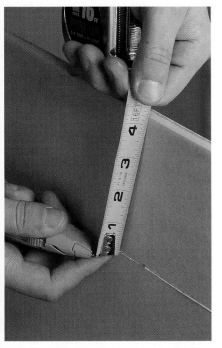

TIP: *Use a steel tape measure as a marking gauge to score wallboard lengthwise when fitting the final row. Hold the blade of a utility knife against the tab at the end of the tape, then guide the tape along the edge of the wallboard.*

9 The final row often requires sheets that are less than full width. Cut sheets to length before cutting to width. After determining the width required, set a wallboard sheet on one long edge so the thinnest piece will be at the top side of the sheet. The thinnest piece may be the "waste" piece—it's easier to cut a sheet when the thinnest piece is on top.

10 Cut and position metal corner bead at the outside corners on areas where the ceiling meets a wall projection, such as a soffit. Press the corner of the bead to flatten the flanges on the wallboard. Drive wallboard nails through the mounting holes and into the framing behind the wallboard. Use wallboard nails, rather than screws, because the heads can be driven flush with the metal surface. Don't drive the nails so far that the metal bead is crimped.

11 Mix joint compound according to the manufacturer's directions. If you use premixed compound, it still needs a quick re-mixing. Don't overmix or you will whip small air bubbles into the compound. The bubbles will pop when the compound is sanded, leaving tiny pits that must be filled with another coat of compound. Use a 6-in. taping knife to spread a layer of joint compound slightly wider than the wallboard tape onto a tapered edge seam, forming a bed for the wallboard tape.

12 Set the end of the wallboard tape into the compound, about 2 in. out from the seam (to leave room for taping the corner). Push the tape forward as you unroll it the length of the seam so it sticks in the compound. About 2 in. from the far end, press the knife firmly into the tape, then tear off the tape against the blade.

13 At the middle of the seam, run the taping knife toward each end of the seam, pressing the tape into the compound and squeezing out extra compound from behind the tape. Press firmly—the surface of the tape should be lower than the surface of the wallboard outside the tapered seam. If there isn't any "squeeze out," you didn't spread a thick enough layer—pull up the tape and begin again.

14 Tape butt joints next. The method is similar to that for tapered seams, but since there isn't a tapered recess, the tape surface will be higher than the wallboard surface. Try to keep the compound and tape layer as thin as possible, but make certain to use enough compound. Begin taping each butt joint at the shoulder of a tapered edge and cut the tape at the shoulder on the other side of the sheet.

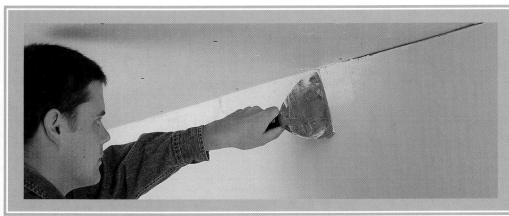

Pre-fill gaps

If you end up with a large gap between the ceiling and wall, fill it with quick-setting joint compound before taping the joint (the quick setting type sets up faster, reducing the amount that it will sag and seep from the gap).

15 Tape the joints where the ceiling meets the walls. Tear the paper tape to length, then fold the tape in the center following the crease. Spread a bed of compound on both sides of the corner (See Tip, above). Begin at one end of the corner and push the tape into the joint, keeping the tape centered.

16 Start in the middle of the joint and use the 6-in. taping knife to press the tape into the compound. Move the knife toward the end of the tape. Do this on both sides of the tape, working your way toward the walls from the middle of the room. When finished, run the knife carefully down each side of the corner to smooth it and clean off any excess compound.

17 Apply a first coat of joint compound, without tape, to the outside corners. Use the taping knife to fill the space between the corner of the metal bead and the wallboard. The knife should rest against the corner of the bead and the wallboard as you pull the knife down the length of the corner. Press firmly so compound penetrates the holes in the corner bead.

19 Use a 12-in. knife to spread compound on either side of the butt joints and for a final, third coat. Since the center of the joint is already higher than the wallboard surface, you need to feather compound farther to hide the high spot. Smooth as with tapered joints. Use the 8-in. knife to spread and feather compound on inside and outside corners. When one side is dry, apply compound to the other side. Use the 6-in. knife at the screw locations. Scrape all the areas of joint compound with a wide knife when they are dry. You want them as smooth as possible before applying the third coat. Stop here if you are texturing the ceiling (See pages 123 to 127).

18 Cover the screw heads in the field. After the joint compound is thoroughly dry, apply the second coat. On tapered seams, use an 8-in. taping knife to spread more joint compound on the seam. Smooth it with a stroke of the knife down each side, then one stroke down the middle. Compound should spread about 2 in. outside the tapered seam on each side and the surface of the compound in the joint should be level with the wallboard surface.

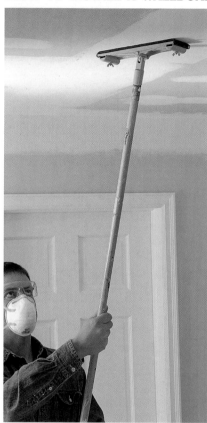

20 Sand the joint compound with a wallboard sanding block and either a sanding screen or sandpaper that's cut to fit the block. Wear a dust mask. Sand until the joint is smooth and level. Edges where compound meets the wallboard surface should be sanded smooth.

Tool Tips

Stilts: Wallboard installers use special stilts, available at rental centers, when taping and applying joint compound on a ceiling. Using the stilts is much quicker than constantly moving a ladder or scaffolding. The working height on the stilts is adjustable and they are surprisingly stable.

Dustless sanders remove most of the sanding dust and make the job less messy. The unit attaches to any shop vacuum and extension handle. The dust is extracted through small holes in the sanding block and caught in the water chamber, which prevents the dust from passing through the vacuum and back into the air. You should still wear a dust mask, and also ear protection for the vacuum noise.

STILTS   **DUSTLESS SANDER**

21 Use a sanding sponge to get a nice crisp edge on the joint where the walls meet the ceiling.

22 Check all the joints for low spots, edges or pits. Further sanding may remove some spots, otherwise apply a light touch-up coat of compound. Sand lightly when dry. Clean the ceiling well, wiping joints with a barely-damp cloth to remove residue. Apply a wallboard primer or latex paint to seal the surface. Then paint or apply other ceiling finish.

Texturizing Ceilings

Spraying a texture compound onto a ceiling is a quick and inexpensive technique for finishing a ceiling. A sprayed texture covers any irregularity less than 1/8 in. in dimension. It allows for a quicker installation of wallboard since it subtracts one round of joint compound application and lessens sanding time. It disguises an uneven ceiling, too, because the textured surface minimizes the shadows and reflections that light makes across a smooth ceiling which highlight blemishes.

There are two basic types of sprayed texture compounds for ceilings. *Pebbled texture* is a mixture of joint compound, white latex paint and small-aggregate particles. When sprayed on the ceiling, it creates a surface covered with tiny "pebbles." Application of this ceiling texture is the quickest because all you have to do is spray it on the ceiling. But it can't be painted later because the pebble-like particles will be knocked off. *Knockdown texture* is a compound resembling thinned joint compound (many professionals make it from just that). It sprays on the ceiling, leaving many different levels of compound. After this sets up for a few minutes, the high points of the texture are flattened with a broad taping knife. This process takes longer and you have to be careful not to leave edges with the taping knife. Knockdown texture can be painted easily after it is dry.

Cover completely any ceiling boxes or duct work openings in the ceiling with plastic. Wear a hat and old clothes or disposable coveralls. Also wear safety glasses, ear protection (from the noise of the power sprayer's air compressor) and a dust mask. Use generous amounts of masking paper, plastic sheeting and tarps. Though most of the texture sticks to the ceiling, it will splatter everywhere. A wide taping knife quickly scrapes it off of wallboard, but finished surfaces should be protected. Clean up carefully—dried texture compound easily crumbles and flakes off masking paper and plastic sheeting. Remove dried spills and splatters of texture compound with a sponge and water.

PHOTO A Texturizing a ceiling has the potential to make an extreme mess, so take the time to prepare by protecting the rest of the room (and the rest of your house) before you start.

PHOTO B Mixing the spray mixture by hand can be a lot of work—simplify the process by using a mixing paddle attachment for an electric drill. For pebble texture (non-paintable) blend dry spray texture mix with water and (if the texture manufacturer suggests) latex-based paint. If you're using knockdown texture, see page 126.

Spray Texture

Only a few tools are needed for spraying a textured ceiling. The power texture sprayer sprays large ceiling areas evenly and easily. It is available for rent at some building centers and at rental centers. A hand-pumped texture sprayer sprays texture on a repaired area. Use a corded drill with a mixing paddle to mix the spray texture compound. The wide taping knife scrapes texture splatters from the walls after spraying, the narrow knife removes dried texture when making a repair. Materials for a spray-textured ceiling include: Self-adhesive masking paper to catch overspray; Plastic sheeting and a tarp to protect wall and floor surfaces from textured compound overspray; Artist's tape (or painter's masking tape) to attach sheeting to wall finishes without risk of tearing the surface; and texturing material—either pebbled texture compound or knockdown texture compound for the ceiling finish desired.

1 For new wallboard, remove joint compound dust from the ceiling using a damp rag. It is not necessary to feather the joint compound absolutely smooth at the joints or screw locations. The line between surface layers less than 1/8 in. apart will not be noticeable after texture is applied. Place a tarp on the floor. Protect flooring with a layer of cardboard underneath the tarp. Then place plastic sheeting over the tarp. It is best if this is one piece, otherwise overlap pieces by several feet. Bunch the sheeting at the foot of the walls (and underneath sheeting on the walls, if used). This will make cleanup much easier. Attach self-adhesive masking paper at the top of the walls around the room **(See Photo A)** to catch most of the texture compound overspray. Protect finished wall surfaces with plastic sheeting long enough to cover the wall down to the floor. It is easier

to tape this in position near the ceiling quickly, using a few pieces of tape, than to use the self-adhesive paper over it. Use artist's tape or painter's masking tape—they won't tear the wall finish.

2 Mix the texturing material according to the manufacturer's instructions. White latex paint is usually added to pebbled texture compound as a bonding agent and to provide a uniform color. Use a heavy-duty corded drill with a mixing paddle attachment—the mixture is very thick **(See Photo B).**

3 Hold the spray gun so the hopper is vertical. Use a small bucket to fill the hopper about three-fourths full with the texture mixture **(See Photo C).** The nozzle control disc on the spray gun may be preset; otherwise set it at the smallest opening that will spray the mixture freely.

4 Hold the spray gun at a 45° angle to the ceiling, 2 to 4 ft. away from the surface. Pull the trigger to spray the mixture onto the ceiling, beginning at a corner. Spray in short bursts while swinging the gun in a wide arc as you move along the ceiling **(See Photo D).** Random movement is better than a rigid pattern. Make certain to spray around all sides of obstacles. Spray as even a coat as possible, but don't backtrack. You can always respray areas that need more texture. Areas that are coated too thickly will sag. The mixture is easily scraped from the ceiling while it is wet if you make a mistake. Respray before the rest of the ceiling dries. Spraying an average 15 × 20-ft. ceiling should take about 30 minutes.

5 If you're applying knockdown texture, let it set for a few minutes, then use a wide taping knife to flatten the top edges of the sprayed texture (See Tip, next page). Work quickly and move the

PHOTO C Load the hopper of the sprayer with well-mixed texture material. Fill it only about three-quarters full at a time. In case of spills, set the hopper and spray mechanism into a bucket before filling. TIP: *Wear disposable coveralls along with face and eye protection.*

PHOTO D Hold the spray gun at about a 45° angle to the ceiling, 2 to 4 ft. away, and spray on the texture. Keep the hopper moving at all times and take care not to apply a layer that's too heavy.

How to texturize a ceiling (continued)

PHOTO E
Clean up the room immediately when you're finished texturizing. Basically, you throw everything into a tarp in the center of the room and collect it into a single bundle.

knife in various directions, being careful not to gouge the texture with the knife's edge.

6 Scrape the overspray from unprotected walls with a wide taping knife. Let the texture dry for about ½ hour. (Remove your shoes before leaving the room—the soles will be coated with texture.)

7 Begin cleanup by removing the self-adhesive masking paper. Pull it from the wall slowly to leave a crisp edge. Wad it into a ball and toss it in the center of the sheeting on the floor. Do the same with plastic sheeting on the walls, if used. Roll up the plastic sheeting on the floor, working from the room edges toward the center **(See Photo E).** Remove splatters or excess texture material from surfaces with a wet sponge. Paint knockdown texture when it is thoroughly dry (24 to 48 hours, depending on humidity).

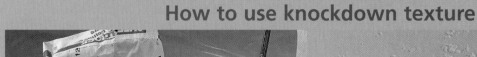

How to use knockdown texture

Combine dry, unaggregated ceiling texture with water in a clean bucket, following the manufacturer's directions. For even blending (and minimal back strain) use a mixing paddle attachment installed in an electric drill to blend the material.

Apply the texture with the power sprayer (See pages 124 to 125) then let it set up for a few minutes. Use a 12-in. taping knife to flatten the top edges of the sprayed texture. Work quickly and move the knife in random directions, being careful not to gouge the texture with the edge of the knife.

Textured ceiling repair in a can

Cans of pressurized spray texture have become quite popular as ceiling repair items in recent years. They spray with quite a bit of force, so before using them, it's a good idea to drape plastic sheeting from the ceiling around the repair area, forming a spray tent. Prepare the ceiling as for a hand pump (See step 1, right) then spray the new texture on. Spray in quarter-second bursts, moving your wrist in a flicking motion.

1 Scrape enough surface smooth around the damaged area so it can be patched, using a 4-in. taping knife. Patch the area as you would patch any wallboard hole (See page 130). Sanding the patched area perfectly smooth isn't necessary

2 To repair the textured surface, we used a small, inexpensive hand pump that can be found at most hardware stores and includes a supply of texture material. After completing the patch, load the texture into the sprayer. Practice spraying on a wallboard scrap to get the feel of the it.

3 Cover the floor and walls. Spray the patched area of the ceiling. Try to get the new material to blend in as best you can. If repairing a ceiling with a knock-down texture, use a wide taping knife to blend the patched area into the surrounding ceiling.

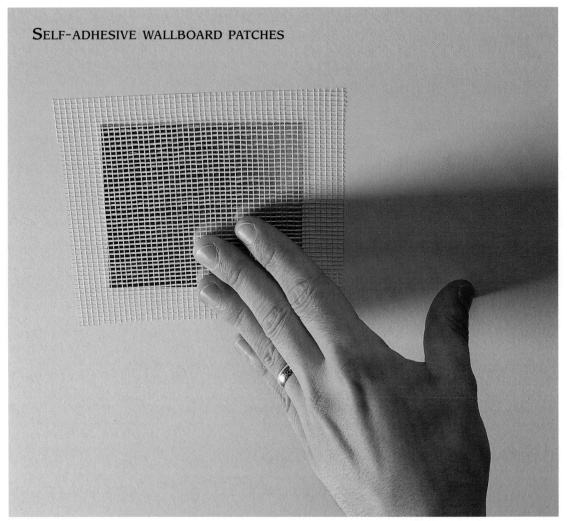

Self-adhesive patches, reinforced with metal mesh, are designed to repair smallish holes that a single patch can cover. Clean off the damaged area, then bond the self-adhesive patch over the hole. Cover with a thin coat of joint compound, feathering the edges to blend in with the surrounding ceiling.

Repairing Wallboard & Plaster Ceilings

Most ceilings aren't in perfect condition. Cracks and small holes are common in plaster ceilings. Small sections may have come loose from the wood lath, or portions of the skim coat may have bubbled or fallen off (often due to water damage). Wallboard ceilings may have nail pops, bubbled seams or water damaged areas. Ceilings also may have holes remaining from removed fixtures, or dents from overly enthusiastic play. But replacing a damaged ceiling is not always necessary. All your ceiling may need is a few repairs.

Repairs to both plaster and wallboard ceilings are relatively simple. They usually involve removal of any damaged or loose material and filling or patching of the remaining dent or hole. Tape and joint compound is used as needed for the filling or patching. See pages 120 to 122 for more information on taping, applying joint compound and sanding. Self-adhesive joint tape is often used for repairs as it is easier to work with, but paper tape is stronger. Use it on larger patches.

Water stains on a ceiling should be treated with a white-pigmented stain sealer. If no damage to the ceiling material has occurred, simply apply the sealer before painting or applying another cosmetic treatment. Otherwise, remove any damaged material before applying sealer and patch as shown below.

If there are more than a few small loose sections, cracks or holes in a plaster ceiling, it may be easier to replace the entire ceiling or install a layer of wallboard over it. Otherwise, more problems may occur after you have finished your remodeling. This is particularly true if your project requires a smooth painted ceiling; it is very difficult to make a flat surface without noticeable blemishes when you've repaired a number of cracks or holes. Reoccurring cracks or cracks that continue to widen in plaster ceilings may indicate a more serious structural problem. You should consult with a professional to determine what repairs are needed.

How to level uneven ceiling joists

An uneven ceiling surface is often very noticeable, especially if the surface is left smooth. Minor irregularities can be hidden with a textured surface or with patterned wallpaper. Use furring strips and shims to level uneven ceiling framing. Determine the lowest point on the ceiling joists, then use a water level to establish level on the other framing based on this point. See page 139 for more information on using a water level.

Staple small pieces of cardboard to the joists for marking the level reference lines. Remember to add in the thickness of the furring strips. Attach the furring strips perpendicular to the ceiling joists. Use shims behind the furring strips at low spots to bring them to level. Because this method lowers ceiling height, you will need to adjust the height of existing electrical boxes. Install wallboard sheets perpendicular to the furring strips.

How to repair a failed wallboard seam

1 Cut out a bubbled or cracked wallboard seam using a utility knife with a sharp blade. Make a "V" wide and deep enough to remove all loose material.

2 Fill the "V" with joint compound, then apply fiber or paper tape. Let dry, then feather layers of joint compound to blend the repair area in with the ceiling.

1 Patch large holes with a piece of wallboard of the same thickness as that on the ceiling. Cut a rectangular patch that is slightly larger than the damaged area, but don't use the tapered edge. Position the patch over the damaged area and trace around the patch. Use a keyhole saw to cut the hole. Caution: Be certain there are no electrical cables or plumbing pipes behind the cutting area.

2 Cut backer strips from scrap ¾-in. plywood sized appropriate to the dimensions of the hole (the backer strips should not flex after installation). Position the backer strips on top of the wallboard and secure by driving wallboard screws through the ceiling and into the backer strips. Take care not to overdrive the screws.

3 Insert the patch into the opening and secure it by driving wallboard screws through the patch and into the backer strips.

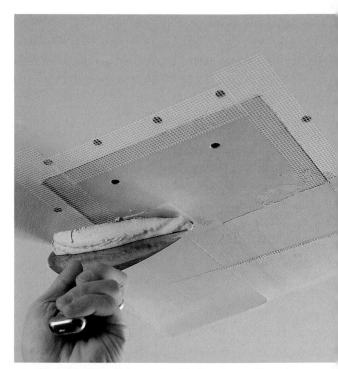

4 Cover the edges of the repair with fiberglass wallboard tape, then coat with joint compound to build up the patch so it is level with the surrounding ceiling surface.

Cracks in plaster

Stabilize a crack in a plaster ceiling with plaster washers. These special screws have a wide, flat flange that holds the plaster tight to the wood lath much better than a regular screw. The flange is perforated to provide better bonding with taping compound.

Note: If you use a power tool to drive the screws, stop about ¼ in. from flush and finish driving the screws by hand. Otherwise, vibrations from the power tool may loosen more plaster.

1 Drive plaster washers on both sides of the crack **(See Photo A),** then check to make certain there is no movement when you press on the ceiling, near the crack.

2 After stabilizing the crack, use a stiff-bladed putty knife or a church-key style bottle opener to open the crack into a "V" shape so it will hold compound **(See Photo B).** Seal the crack with white pigmented sealer. This helps bond joint compound to the plaster.

3 Apply self-adhesive wallboard repair tape over the crack, then cover the tape with joint compound **(See Photo C).** Use a fast-setting compound for the first coat, as it doesn't shrink and dries harder than regular compound. If the crack is deeper or wider than ¼ in., seal it, then fill it just shy of the ceiling surface with a coat of fast setting compound. This will make certain that the crack is filled properly. After the compound dries, apply tape and regular joint compound. Sand until the repair blends in with the rest of the ceiling.

For a plaster repair method for more extensive cracks, see pages 134 to 135.

HOW TO REPAIR CRACKS IN PLASTER

PHOTO A Drive special "plaster washer" screws through the ceiling surface and into the lath on both sides of the crack to stabilize it. Finish driving the screws with a hand screwdriver to prevent damage from vibrations.

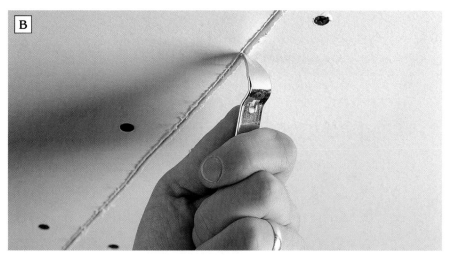

PHOTO B Clean out the crack and create a bonding surface by scraping the crack with a bottle opener or a putty knife.

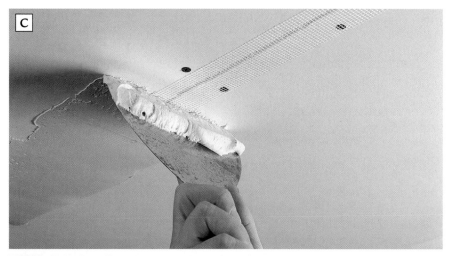

PHOTO C Apply wallboard tape over the seam (self-adhesive fiberglass tape is shown here) then apply joint compound over the tape and blend it in with the rest of the ceiling.

HOW TO REPAIR A SMALL HOLE IN PLASTER

PHOTO A Scrape the damaged area with a wire brush to remove any loose debris and to expose solid plaster.

PHOTO B Apply quick-setting joint compound into the hole with a putty knife. Sand smooth after the compound has dried.

Repairing small holes in plaster (above)

1 Remove loose material from the damaged area. Scrape and use a steel brush vigorously to remove all damaged plaster and dust to ensure a good bond for repair materials. If only surface layers of plaster are missing, use a stiff-bladed 3-in. putty knife to carve cross-hatching into the remaining plaster to provide some "tooth" to help hold the repair compound **(See Photo A).** Brush away remaining plaster dust. Seal the repair area with white-pigmented sealer.

2 Spread and feather layers of joint compound to blend the repair area into the rest of the ceiling **(See Photo B).** If the hole is more than ¼ in. deep, first use fast-setting joint compound to fill the area just shy of the plaster surface; let it dry, then finish with regular compound.

3 For small holes where wood lath is exposed, follow steps A and B above, then fill the hole just shy of the plaster surface with fast-setting compound. Make certain to force the compound into the lath so it pushes through the spaces between lath pieces, locking the patch to the lath. When the compound dries, finish patching with regular compound.

Repairing larger holes in plaster (right page)

1 Use a piece of ⅜-in. wallboard to patch large holes. Cut a rectangular piece of wallboard slightly larger than the damaged area from wallboard that isn't thicker than the plaster. Do not use the tapered edge. Trace around the wallboard onto the plaster **(See Photo C).**

2 Use a fixed-blade utility knife with a sharp blade to score through the skim coat on all the lines **(See Photo D).** This will dull the blade, but it then can be used to carve through the base coats until you reach the lath. This method takes time and elbow grease, but prevents any further loosening of plaster that a saw or hammer and chisel can cause.

3 Seal the plaster edges with white pigmented sealer. Attach the wallboard patch to the lath with screws. Shim behind the wallboard if necessary, but the face of the patch should not extend past the plaster surface **(See Photo E).** It is fine if it is slightly shy of the plaster surface as this depression is easily filled with joint compound.

4 Tape the repair and apply joint compound **(See Photo F).**

HOW TO REPAIR A LARGE HOLE IN PLASTER

PHOTO C Cut a square patch slightly larger than the damaged area from a scrap of wallboard. Position the patch over the damaged area and trace the edges onto the ceiling.

PHOTO D Remove the plaster, but not the lath, from the damaged area using a sharp utility knife.

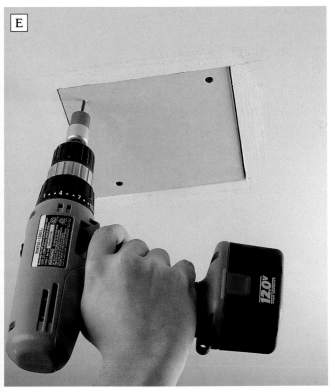

PHOTO E Insert the patch into the opening created in the damaged area and secure it to the lath with wallboard screws.

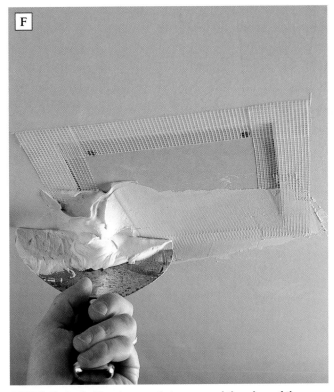

PHOTO F Apply fiberglass repair tape around the edges of the repair, then cover with quick-setting joint compound (you'll probably need two or three thin layers for a smooth, crack-free surface).

Plaster Repair Membrane

Back in my remodeling days, I spent a few months doing apartment restorations in historic buildings. One of the biggest challenges was repairing cracked plaster. I fixed what I could with fiberglass tape and joint compound, but sometimes walls and ceilings had so many cracks that I installed ¼-in. drywall over the plaster. This usually created problems trying to make the trim reveals look right, and all of the outlet boxes ended up being recessed, but there was no better approach at the time. Today there is.

The Nu-Wal restoration system from Specification Chemicals is different from any other plaster repair product I've seen. You cover the plaster ceiling or walls with elastomeric coating and fiberglass mat. They provide a continuous resilient surface that cracks won't telegraph through over time. The system also helps prevent future cracking.

Once the coating cures, it looks similar to primed drywall. You can paint it with ordinary paint or wallpaper it. It is not recommended over wallpaper or wood paneling. They won't allow the elastomeric coating to stick properly.

Before starting, cover the floor with a dropcloth. Remove loose paint and plaster from the wall

1 Remove loose paint and plaster. Fill large cracks and sand sharp edges so they don't telegraph through.

2 After snapping a 4-ft. reference line, apply the base coat of saturant using a medium-nap roller.

3 Cut the mat 2 in. longer than needed. Press with a dry roller or wallpaper brush to eliminate air bubbles. Wear a NIOSH-approved respirator.

4 Trim the mat to length. Don't try to cover the wall and ceiling with one piece.

with a scraper or broadknife. Scrape or sand cracks smooth to minimize ridges that may telegraph through the mat. Clean away grease, dirt and dust. Fill any cracks wider than $1/16$ in. with drywall compound and sand the patches smooth after it dries.

Spot-prime any patched spots or bare plaster to prevent them from absorbing the coating too quickly. If plaster is chalky, you

must seal it with a penetrating sealer before applying the coating.

Mark vertical lines on the walls at 4-ft. intervals to provide a reference so you don't coat too big an area at one time.

The nonwoven fiberglass mat uses a jackstraw pattern that can release tiny glass fibers into the air when you handle or brush it. The mat may remind you of wallpaper, but you should handle it with the

5 Cover the mat with a second coat of the saturant, making sure to embed the mat firmly into the base coat.

6 After coating the mat evenly, continue rolling the base coat onto the adjacent 4-ft. section of wall.

7 Apply sections of mat with a 1-in. overlap. Double-cut the seam with the knife 45° down and to the side.

8 Remove the two strips of excess mat and smooth the seam. Then apply saturant to the seam and the uncoated mat.

same care you would fiberglass insulation. Seal off the room from the rest of the house and, if possible, ventilate the work area with a large window fan directed outdoors. I overlooked the manufacturer's cautions printed on the box and failed to wear the recommended NIOSH-approved respirator and gloves. As a result, I paid the price coughing and itching all night after finishing the job.

Using this system is similar to installing wallpaper. To begin, cut the mat off the roll in lengths 2 in. longer than needed. Precut a number of pieces, because once you get started, there's no good time to stop and cut more strips. Apply the elastomer saturant with a medium-nap (⅜-in.) roller. This allows you to spread on a heavy enough coat to embed the mat. Affix the fiberglass mat to the wet

surface, pressing it into the coating with a dry paint roller or a wallpaper brush. The manufacturer says the roller works best for eliminating air bubbles and minimizing the release of glass fibers.

Once the mat is stuck, trim it at the ceiling and base with a sharp utility knife or razor knife. Trim the mat around any outlets or switches in the wall, being careful not to touch the knife to live wires or devices.

After installing and trimming the mat, apply a second coat of elastomeric coating, saturating the fiberglass evenly. Immediately apply the base coat to the next 4-ft. section. Install a second strip of mat, overlapping the first piece by about an inch. Make the seam cut with a sharp utility knife or razor knife at a 45° side bevel. Cut with the tip of the knife pointed toward the uncoated sheet you just installed to ensure that the joint will lap in the proper orientation. The cut doesn't need to be perfect; as long as you slice through both sheets at one time, they will match perfectly. After the material dries, the seam will disappear.

Trim the mat at inside and outside corners. When you apply the second coat of elastomer, it will fill the small gap. Don't attempt to wrap the corners as you would with wallpaper. It's almost impossible to keep the sheet from wrinkling if you do.

Nu-Wal not only restores cracked plaster but also encapsulates lead paint. If you seal the mat tightly at the edges, the system also acts as a vapor barrier for exterior walls and ceilings. Once the material cures, you can paint or finish it as you like, including using it as a substrate for wall tile.

The #2500 saturant covers 80 sf per gallon (base and finish coats). We finished four walls and the ceiling of a 9 × 11-ft. room with 9-ft. ceilings and had material to spare.

~ Blake Stranz

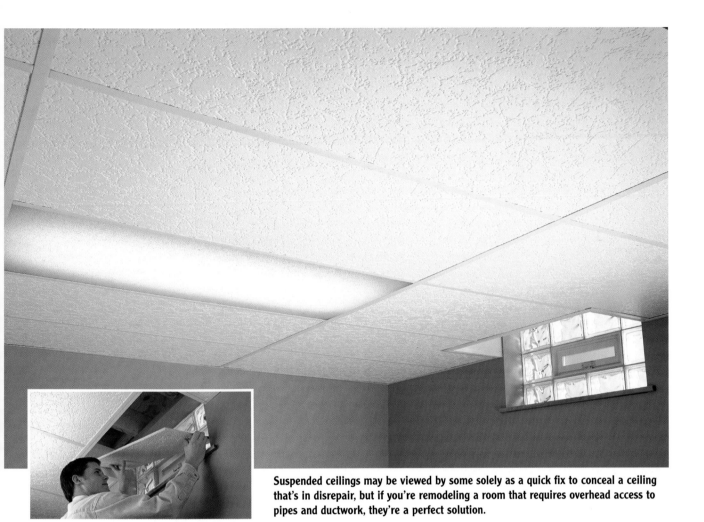

Suspended ceilings may be viewed by some solely as a quick fix to conceal a ceiling that's in disrepair, but if you're remodeling a room that requires overhead access to pipes and ductwork, they're a perfect solution.

Suspended Ceilings

A suspended ceiling is useful when permanent access to the ceiling area behind it is needed; for example, if you're remodeling a basement and the plumbing, electrical or ductwork must remain accessible. The most common installation is a grid framework made of lightweight metal brackets hung beneath the existing ceiling surface or joists. Pieces of ceiling panel are placed on the flanges of the brackets, filling the open spaces in the grid between the brackets. The panels are easily removed when access is needed, and then quickly replaced when work is finished. A suspended ceiling also is a simple and relatively inexpensive way to convert a room with a high ceiling to a standard 8-ft. ceiling height or cover over a damaged ceiling surface.

A minimum space of 4 in. must be left behind the suspended ceiling framework so the panel pieces can be placed in or taken out of the brackets. Keep this in mind when deciding if a suspended ceiling is right for your project, as this significant change in ceiling height can affect the function of doors, lighting fix-

tures, wall cabinets and shelving. Plus, many building codes have minimum ceiling height regulations that could apply to a suspended ceiling installation. Check with your local building inspector about any restrictions for your project.

Suspended ceiling panels are available in 2 × 2 or 2 × 4-ft. sections. Fluorescent light fixtures designed to fit within the grid framework also are available. Or you can use standard incandescent and recessed light fixtures in the suspended ceiling, though their installation will require some adaptation to fit the suspended ceiling height. Consult with your local building inspector if you aren't confident about your ability to make these electrical installations.

You will need to determine joist locations if installing a suspended ceiling in a room with an existing ceiling surface. Runners should be installed perpendicular to the ceiling joists and the support wires for the metal framework must be attached to the joists. If the ceiling joists are visible, remember that a minimum of 4 in. of space must be available beneath the lowest structural members, pipes or cables in the ceiling area.

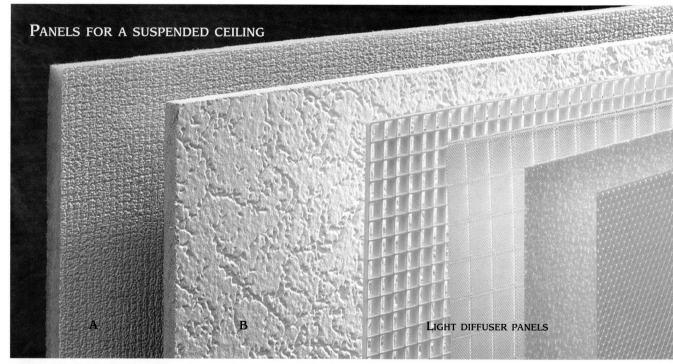

PANELS FOR A SUSPENDED CEILING

A   B   LIGHT DIFFUSER PANELS

Common ceiling and diffuser panels include:
Insulated panels (A); Acoustical tiles (B) that dampen the sound in a room. Light diffuser panels come in a wide range of styles and opacities. They are designed to fit into a grid with 2 × 4-ft. openings, in conjunction with a 4-ft.-long fluorescent light fixture.

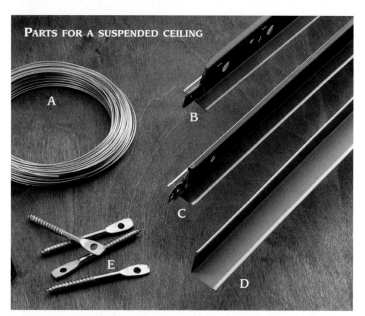

PARTS FOR A SUSPENDED CEILING

A common suspended ceiling system includes: Wall angle pieces (D) that are attached to the walls around the room's perimeter; Runners (B) rest on the wall angles at the ends of the room and are supported by wires attached to the ceiling joists; Cross-tees (C) attach between the runners (or between runners and wall angles at the sides of the room) and complete the grid sections for the ceiling panels; Screw eyes (E) are attached to the ceiling joists to hang support wires (A) that are cut to length and hold up the grid framework.

Purchasing Tips: *Choose a suspended ceiling system with lightweight metal brackets. Some systems use plastic hardware that is not as durable. Also choose a system where a level ceiling is established during installation. Systems that attach directly to the existing ceiling or joists (designed to save ceiling height) may look uneven, depending on the irregularity of the existing surfaces, plus they may not allow enough access space for the mechanical systems in the ceiling area.*

Ceiling tiles

Ceiling tiles (also called acoustical tiles) are a similar product to ceiling panels, but usually come in 12 × 12-in. pieces. They are glued or stapled to the ceiling surface or to furring strips attached to joists, or they can be clipped into metal tracks attached to the ceiling. Because they are permanently attached, ceiling tiles can't be used where ceiling access is necessary. But they will cover a damaged ceiling surface, provide sound dampening in noisy rooms and offer decorative possibilities.

Water levels

A water level is an indispensable tool for marking a level line around the perimeter of a room. A water level is a long, clear plastic hose containing water, with an electronic unit at one end. The electronic unit is fixed at the desired level height. The free end of the hose is raised at locations all around the room until the electronic unit signals with a beep when level is reached. This makes it simple to use by yourself, especially since it works around corners, too.

Suspended ceiling

You can install a suspended ceiling by yourself, but it will be much easier if you have a helper. Be sure you work on stable ladders and that the power is turned off to any electrical circuits on which you must work. Establish a layout where the runners are aligned with the length of the room and perpendicular to the ceiling joists. If the room requires less than full panels to complete length or width, balance the layout so trimmed panel pieces of equal dimension fall on opposite sides of the room.

1 Mark the planned ceiling height in one corner of the room **(See Photo A).** Allow at least 4 in. clearance between the brackets and the ceiling or joists, or any exposed pipes or ductwork (whichever is lower). In some cases, obstacles such as a support beam or a low duct can be worked around so you don't have to lower your entire ceiling by 6 inches just to cover a lone furnace duct (ask your local building department). To avoid these obstacles, box them in with furring strips and wallboard, then work them into the grid layout as if they were walls.

2 A water level is the perfect tool for establishing level reference lines around a room (See *Water Levels,* previous page). Attach the electronic unit end of the water level to the wall in the corner so the indicator arrow on the casing is aligned with the ceiling height mark.

3 Place the free end of the water level in the corner at the opposite end of the wall from the electronic unit. It doesn't matter if tubing remains coiled or rests on the floor, as long as no tubing lies above the two ends of the level. Move the end of the hose until you hear the beep indicating level has been reached. Mark this height on

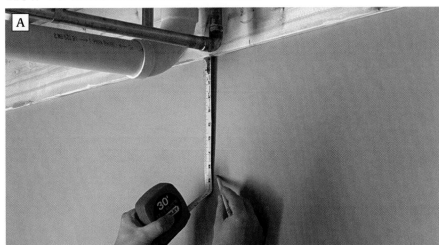

PHOTO A Measure down at least 4 in. from the lowest point of the ceiling or joist area. Mark a reference point (the point should be at least 84 in. above the floor in most areas). Use this point as a base for creating additional reference points and lines.

PHOTO B Mark level reference points all around the room to guide the installation of the suspended grid. The height marks should be at the planned ceiling height plus the thickness of the grid members (¾ in. in our case). We used a water level as a guide.

PHOTO C Snap a chalkline to connect the reference marks and create reference lines.

PHOTO D Frame in openings, such as this basement window, by building a wood box (called a valance) that projects out from the wall far enough to allow light in and to meet minimum clearance standards for windows (check with your building department).

PHOTO E Attach the wall-mounted angle pieces to the wall (and valances or boxed-in obstructions). Make miter joints at the corners.

PHOTO F Mark locations for the grid members (called "runners" and "cross-tees") on the wall angle pieces. Snap chalklines between opposing marks to lay out the grid lines on the joists or the old ceiling.

both sides of the corner. These marks will be level with the first marks made at the other end of the wall. Make marks every 4 ft. along all walls, using the original height mark as a reference for the electronic unit **(See Photo B).**

4 After marking the ceiling height (plus grid track thickness) around the perimeter, snap alignment lines between the marks **(See Photo C).**

5 Box around openings, such as basement windows, that are higher on the wall than the new ceiling height. Build a valance out of 1× lumber to surround the opening, providing clearance from the suspended ceiling. The bottom of the valance should be flush with the planned height of the bottom of the ceiling **(See Photo D).** Since the method for making and installing the valance depends largely on the characteristics of the opening and the structure of the ceiling, you'll need to rely on your carpentry skills to figure out the best strategy for your house.

6 Attach wall angle pieces to the studs on all walls **(See Photo E).** We used 1¼ in. wallboard screws. The tops of the angle pieces should be flush with the reference line. Also attach angle pieces (at the same height) to valances or boxed-in obstructions, Miter-cut the corners with metal snips.

TIP: *Use short masonry nails driven into the mortar joints to attach wall angles to concrete block walls.*

7 Mark the location of the runner pieces on the wall angles, depending on the size of ceiling panels you are using. Arrange the runners so any cut panels will be balanced at each end, much the same way you would plan a tile layout. Using the runner marks as references, snap a chalkline across the ceiling, above the position of

each runner **(See Photo F).** The runners should be parallel to one another and perpendicular to the end walls for proper installation.

8 Determine the placement of the cross-tees using the same principles as with the runners (try to minimize cuts, conserve on materials and create a balanced layout). Since most runners are preformed with slots for the cross-tees spaced at 2-ft. intervals, once you've established one cross-tee location the rest will set themselves automatically (provided that you locate the runners so the slots are aligned). Locate the first cross-tee somewhere near the starting wall, then drive nails into wall studs at opposite walls, flush with the bottom of the wall angles. Tie mason's string between the opposing nails so it is taut, establishing a reference line **(See Photo G).**

9 Drive a screw through a support-wire screw eye and into a ceiling joist every 4 ft. along the chalklines marking the runner hanger locations. Bend the free end of the wires so they hang at least 5 in. below the mason's string level **(See Photo H).** Trim the excess off if it is in the way.

10 Install the runners by setting the ends on the wall angles at the location marks. Make sure that a cross-tee slot on each runner aligns with the reference line. Splice runner pieces together as you raise them into place **(See Photo I),** if necessary, following manufacturer's directions. Make certain that the slots for the cross-tees are aligned between runners and with their location marks on the wall angles (running a mason's string between the first cross-tee marks is helpful). Trim the runners to adjust for partial panels at either end. You may have to trim off of both ends, or trim more from one end than the other to keep the cross-tee slots aligned.

PHOTO G Determine the best location for the cross-tees, then mark one cross-tee location by driving nails at the ends of the room and snapping a chalkline.

PHOTO H Bend the support wires for the runners and cross-tees at a consistent height to ensure that the ceiling grid is level.

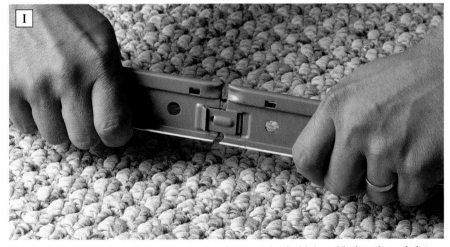

PHOTO I Make splices in the runners by forming a mechanical joint with the tabs and slots formed at the ends of the pieces.

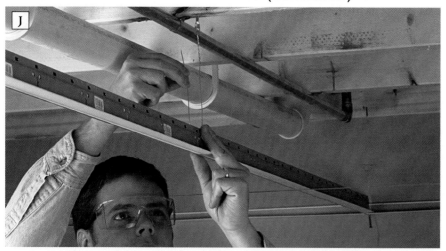

PHOTO J Hang the runners from the support wires, using the mason's strings as guides. Make sure to position a guide wire as close as possible to each end of a splice.

PHOTO K Snap the cross-tees in place between runners and between the end runners and the wall angle pieces.

PHOTO L Install light fixtures before installing the ceiling panels. Mounting clips are used to attach this 4-ft. fluorescent fixture to the cross-tees at the ends of the opening. Wires attached to the joists or ceiling can be used for additional support.

11 Attach the free ends of the wires to the runners, twisting to secure them **(See Photo J)**. Make certain the bottoms of the runners are level with the mason's strings. If a support wire isn't within a few inches of a splice between runner pieces, attach a support wire to the nearest joist and connect the wire to a runner as close as possible to the splice.

12 Attach the cross-tees to the runners **(See Photo K)**. If a cross-tee is cut to fit a partial panel, rest the cut end on the wall angle.

13 Install ceiling fixtures, following manufacturer's directions **(See Photo L)**. Usually, this involves screwing mounting brackets to the runners. Mount the fixture on the brackets, then attach wires to the fixture to support its weight. After connecting the electrical wires and installing the light tubes, place the translucent diffuser cover into the grid.

Recessed light fixtures: Measure, mark and cut carefully for recessed light fixtures. This usually requires splitting the ceiling panel at the center of the cutout. Then, each partial panel can be placed into position. Cut the opening in the panel (but don't split the panel), then raise the can to its highest setting. Place a ceiling panel from an adjacent opening, sliding it under the light fixture. Lower the can into position and attach the fixture trim.

14 Place the full ceiling panels into the grid **(See Photo M)**. Use a straightedge and sharp utility knife to trim partial panels to size **(See Photo N)**. Cut panels with the finished surface up.

15 Fill in exposed joists or old ceiling areas, such as the area above a valance, by cutting a piece of ceiling panel to fit and bonding it in place with construction adhesive **(See Photo O)**.

PHOTO M Install the full ceiling panels first, slipping each panel up into the opening formed in the grid, then letting it settle down onto the ledges of the runners and cross-tees. You may need to help it a bit by reaching in through an adjacent opening and pushing down on the panel from above.

PHOTO N Cut ceiling panels by slicing all the way through with a utility knife. Cut them face-side up so the face isn't marred by tear-out. Use a straightedge to guide your cut—a scrap of a runner works well.

PHOTO O Patch in openings above valances by cutting a piece of a ceiling panel to fit and bonding it to the joist or ceiling at the top of the opening with construction adhesive.

Once a common ceiling covering, pressed and embossed metal ceilings are enjoying a resurgence in popularity.

Metal Panel Ceilings

Pressed metal ceiling panels (also known as embossed metal panels) give character and individuality to a room. Patterned after the tin ceilings of the late 1800s, this product is available at some home centers or by mail order from companies found in home building and remodeling magazines, as well as over the Internet.

The original tin ceilings were a cheaper and more practical substitute for ornate plaster or woodwork. The modern version offers a wide variety of design possibilities. Depending on the manufacturer, you can find dozens of patterns, with metal cornices and mold-ing to mix or match. Filler panels also are available as an option for filling the area between full panel pieces and the ceiling perimeter. You can paint these pressed metal ceiling pieces to resemble elaborate plasterwork at a fraction of the cost. Pressed metal panels can be used for wainscoting or wall panels. You also can combine metal panels with wood cove moldings or other trim.

Besides the decorative possibilities, one advantage of a metal ceiling is its ability to easily, permanently and relatively inexpensively cover over a problem ceiling area. For example, you can install metal ceiling panels instead of patching a maze of cracks and holes in a plaster ceiling, or instead of steaming, stripping and scraping wallpaper from a poorly primed ceiling.

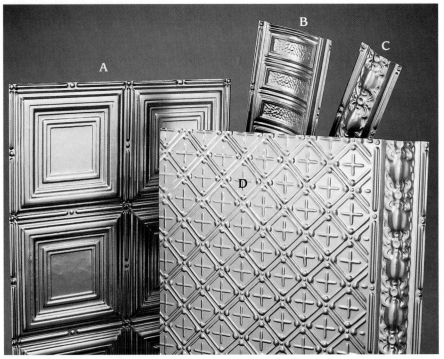

A typical metal ceiling installation requires a few different panel and trim types. Field panels (A) are used for the field area; Cornice trim (B) is installed like crown molding to transition from ceiling to wall; Molding strips (C) are used to create a decorative border between the field panels and the cornice; Filler strips (D) are also installed between the field panels and the cornice. Some, like the one shown here, have a molding strip pressed into the edge.

Handling & finishing metal panels

Wear work gloves when handling metal panels and cornice trim. Their edges are sharp enough to cut skin, plus skin oils on the raw metal can cause stains that will blemish the surface, even under a coat of polyurethane. Clean the metal pieces with denatured alcohol and let dry. Seal the backsides of each piece with a coat of clear polyurethane or primer, depending on which finish you will use for the finished side. Let dry thoroughly. Coat the panels and any cornice, molding and filler pieces with polyurethane if you want to retain the silvery finish. If you are painting the metal pieces, you may want to caulk the overlapped seams that you have sealed to make a completely smooth finish before priming and painting. Make certain to use a caulk compatible with the primer and paint.

Standard sizes for metal ceiling panels are 2 × 2, 2 × 4 or 2 × 8 ft., depending on the pattern and the manufacturer. The panels have round catches, called beads, that fit into one another to properly align the pieces where they overlap. These beads also serve as nailing points for attaching the panels to the ceiling surface. Most manufacturers provide 1-in. cone-head nails for attaching the panels to the nailing surface, but you can use flathead nails instead.

Determine a layout that will look balanced but will use the fewest number of panels, to make installation easier and to minimize expense. Keep in mind the size of the cornice or other molding you will use when determining the layout of the panel pieces.

It is best to work with a helper because of the size and flexibility of the metal panels. They can bend and crease easily if not supported during installation. A coat of polyurethane should be applied to the panels to retain the original silvery tin color (otherwise they will tarnish). Or paint the panels according to your decorating scheme (make certain you apply a metal-compatible primer and paint).

Common layouts for metal ceiling panels include:
• Completely covering the ceiling with metal panels and installing a metal cornice or wood crown or cove moldings. Begin installation with full panel pieces in the corner of the room farthest from the entrance, causing any partial panels to fall on the two least noticeable sides of the room.
• Creating a centered section of full panels bordered with molding pieces. The ceiling surface between the molding and the cornice can be completed with filler pieces, painted or covered with wallpaper.

How to Install a Metal Panel Ceiling

1 Install a nailing surface for the metal panels out of 4 × 8 sheets of ½-in. construction-grade plywood. Lay out the plywood so the long edges of the sheets are perpendicular to the joists and the end seams are staggered. Attach the plywood to the ceiling joists with screws long enough to penetrate any existing ceiling surface and at least 1½ in. into the joists. Drive screws every 6 in. and every 12 in. (at joist locations) in the field area.

2 Begin installing the metal panels at the corner farthest from the room's entrance. Snap a chalkline perpendicular to the end wall at the correct distance for the long edge of the first row of panels (See Tip, next step). Remember to allow for the depth of any cornice or molding pieces before snapping this line.

TIP: *To create a line on the ceiling perpendicular to a wall, use the 3-4-5 right triangle principle. Mark the intersection of the ceiling and wall where you want the line to begin. Make a mark 3 ft. from this corner along the wall/ceiling intersection. Make another mark 4 ft. from the corner along the ceiling in the direction the line will take. The distance on the diagonal between these last two marks should be 5 ft. If it isn't, adjust the mark on the ceiling until there is exactly 5 ft. between the two marks. Snap a chalkline from the corner through this ceiling mark, creating the perpendicular line.*

3 Position the first panel so its long edge is aligned with the perpendicular chalkline. Drive a 1-in. conehead nail at the side of a bead (where it will be covered by the overlapping panel piece) in the middle and at the corners of this long edge. Nail down the center of the panel every 12 in. at a bead location. Drive the nails through the center of the bead. Then, nail down the rest of the edges with nails driven through the center of the bead every 6 in. Drive nails to the sides of the beads in the middle and at the corners of an edge wherever there will be an overlapping panel or cornice piece.

4 Position the next panel at the end of the first piece, with the beads interlocking (like a ball-and-socket joint). Make certain the long edge of the panel is aligned with the chalkline. Nail down the center of the panel, then nail the edges. Drive nails through bead centers every 6 in. along the edge overlapping the first panel.

5 Complete installing the first row of panels. Trim the last panel piece to length, if necessary, using straight metal snips. Be careful—the metal edges are very sharp.

6 When making a cutout within a panel, make a starter hole for your metal shears by placing a scrap piece of wood underneath the panel and drilling overlapping ½-in.-dia. starter holes inside the cutout outline. Several starter holes may be necessary to make cutting easier. Use curved metal snips for cutouts with curved outlines. Install the panel after the cutouts are made.

7 Begin installing the second row by attaching a panel adjacent to the first panel in the first row. Line up the beads at the long edges. Drive nails through the center of the panel, then along the edges. Attach the panel at the sides of beads at the middle and corners of edges that will be overlapped by another piece, and through the bead centers every 6 in. on finished edges.

8 Complete the installation of all the metal panels, row by row. Seal the overlapping panel edges by tapping a small block of wood against the edges until they touch the underlying panel. NOTE: Install filler pieces now, if you need them: Measure and trim to fit the area between the full panel pieces and the ceiling edges, allowing for cornice and molding dimensions. Attach the fillers to the ceiling in the same manner as the panel pieces.

9 Install any molding pieces (these usually come in 4-ft. lengths). Overlap them, as with the flat ceiling panels, nailing every 6 in. and sealing the edges. Before installing, mark and cut 45° miters in one of the ends of molding pieces that meeting at inside corners—you won't be able to mark the trim once mating pieces are installed.

10 Attach the cornice pieces, nailing at every wall stud and every 6 in. on the ceiling. So the mitered cornice piece can form to the profile of the straight-cut cornice piece, make 1/8-in.-deep cuts 1/8 in. apart in the mitered edge. Seal the overlapping edges.

11 At outside corners, you'll need to miter-cut both cornice pieces. Mark the ceiling on both sides of a corner using a scrap piece of cornice held in position, showing where the pieces will intersect. Use these reference marks to indicate where to mark for miter cuts on both cornice pieces, then make the cuts. Snip the mitered edge of one piece with 1/8-in.-deep cuts 1/8 in. apart. After installing, tap the head of a nail against these small tabs to seal the miter. Apply a protective finish to the ceiling (See page 146).

Installing crown molding and cornices is a relatively tricky process, but the payoff is high if your goal is a room with a more formal appearance.

Ceiling Trim

Trim molding can be an elegant addition to just about any ceiling. While the complex profiles, angles and large sizes of many moldings make their installation one of the most complicated trim carpentry projects, the beautiful results make the work worthwhile. Most ceiling molding, such as crown molding, is "sprung." A sprung molding is a wide, thin piece installed at an angle to the ceiling and wall surfaces, leaving a triangular hollow space behind the molding. Molding with simple, flat profiles can be installed at ceilings the same way baseboard is installed. Or, you may use cornice assemblies made of multiple profiles.

Ceilings and walls that are out of square make installing molding particularly tricky and time consuming. If your remodeling project requires removal of wall and ceiling surfaces or involves new construction, extra time spent squaring the framing will make molding work much easier. Unless you have fine carpentry experience, it is best to let a professional install a complex cornice assembly or very wide crown molding (usually over 4½ in. wide) that can't be cut in your power miter box. Even when using a compound miter saw, cutting these moldings requires complex math formulas. A simple solution is to install complex molding with preformed corners and straight sections (See Tip, page 156).

When planning your ceiling trim project, determine an installation sequence requiring the fewest mitered and coped joints. Then calculate how many lineal feet of molding is required. Make certain to allow enough at outside corners—wider moldings project further away from the corner, requiring more material. Also, unless you are installing a flat, baseboard-like type of ceiling molding, purchase about 15 to 20% of extra material. You will need more because of the fitting techniques required when installing crown moldings. Plan for this extra amount by adding an extra foot for each coped or mitered end to each piece when purchasing lengths of molding. If you decide to have molding custom-milled, make certain to purchase plenty of stock. It is often very expensive to have a small amount made if you run out.

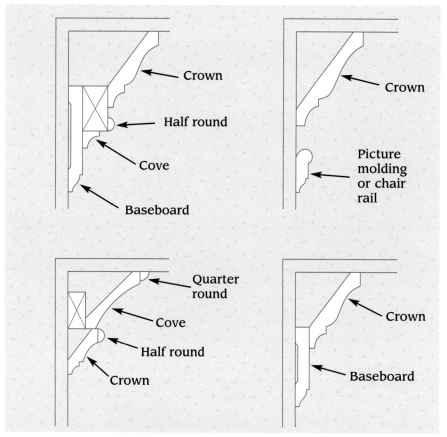

Cornice molding is usually a combination of separate molding profiles assembled together at the ceiling (four common combinations are shown above). This is most often a treatment for a formal room. Because the final unit often uses one or more crown moldings, flat moldings and extra nailing surfaces, building a cornice molding is very involved and time consuming. But cutting joints and installing the pieces to form a cornice are done with the same methods as those shown in the crown molding installation.

Tool Tip: The compound miter saw

For cutting sprung moldings, nothing beats a compound miter saw. Because they adjust on both a horizontal and vertical plane they can be set up to handle both the bevel and the miter cut without the need to use jigs or make adjustments to the table or fence. Many have positive stops for cutting standard-size crown and cove molding miters.

Tips for installing ceiling trim

• The easiest installation will have each run of molding along the ceiling made from one piece, rather than splicing shorter pieces together with a scarf joint (See page 109).

• Install the longest piece of molding opposite the entryway to the room. This piece should have a butt joint at each end so the coped joints of the molding pieces meeting it won't be noticed if seasonal movement causes them to open up. As a rule, you will have a much easier installation when a butt joint is used on at least one end of as many molding pieces as possible.

• Don't finish the project sequence with a molding piece requiring mitered or coped joints on both ends, if possible, particularly in rooms that are out of square.

• Use nails long enough to penetrate about 1½ in into the joists.

• A pneumatic finish nail gun will greatly speed up a molding installation. Positioning and nailing the molding is much easier and quicker, plus the gun automatically sets the nail-head below the surface of the wood. Finish nail guns will shoot finish nails up to 3 in. long and are available at rental centers.

• Fill nail holes with wood putty and fill any gaps in joints with caulk (caulk is better than putty because it flexes).Then, prime and paint. If you're applying a clear wood finish, stain molding before installation—unless you apply stain with a sprayer, in which case follow the same procedure as for painting. Fill nail holes and gaps with color-matched putty applied after staining. Cut and install molding before painting.

HOW TO INSTALL CROWN MOLDING

1 Outfit your power miter saw with a simple crown molding jig (no jig is needed with a compound miter saw—See Tool Tip, previous page). The three elements of the jig are a fence, table and a stop. The goal is to join these parts so they are square and the stop is positioned on the table so it holds the crown molding in the same relationship to the fence that the wall has with the ceiling: When resting in the jig, the flat surfaces on the back of the crown molding should be flush against the fence and the stop. Make clearance cuts in the fence for the saw blade. Screw the jig to the saw fence.

2 Cut three 2-ft.-long pieces of molding to use as templates for laying out joints. Place the molding upside down in the jig. Using the crown molding jig, cut mating 45° bevels at the ends of two of the templates. On the third, make a square butt cut.

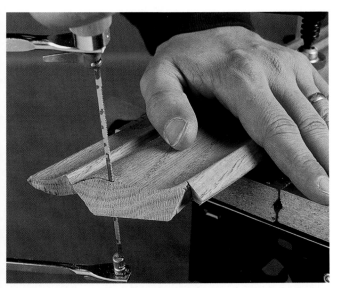

3 Cut the cope in each mitered template piece, using a coping saw held at an angle to the backside of the molding. For thick molding, hold the coping saw roughly at 80° to the backside; for thin molding use a 60° angle. (Some of this depends on the profile of the molding. You may need to experiment to determine the best coping saw angle—some parts of the profile may require cutting at a different angle than others.) This creates a back cut, causing the edge of the finished cut to match the profile of the mating trim piece. Label the templates.

4 Use the square-cut template as a guide to draw reference lines at each outside corner in the room. Simply hold the template squarely against the wall and ceiling so the end extends past the corner a few inches. From each side of the corner, trace the edge of the template where it meets the ceiling. The point where the reference lines meet will represent the top of the miter joint when formed.

5 Use a water level to transfer a level reference point around the tops of all walls (See pages 138 to 139 for more information on using water levels). The distance from the ceiling should represent the bottom of the crown molding when installed (use one of the template pieces to find this distance). Snap a chalkline connecting the marks to establish a guide line for positioning the bottom of the crown molding. Measure from the chalkline to the ceiling in at several spots. If no spot is more than ⅜ in. out of level, proceed with the installation. For ceilings more than ⅜ in. out of level, adjust the chalkline so it is properly positioned relative to the lowest point. Shims will be necessary to fill the gap between molding and ceiling at nailing points. When installation is complete, use caulk to fill gaps that are less than 3 ft. long. Use joint compound to feather the ceiling level for longer gaps (See TIP, page 156).

6 Cut and install the first molding piece, based on the installation sequence. This should be a long piece with butt joints at each end. Cut the piece ¹⁄₁₆ in. longer than necessary and back-cut the butt cuts slightly. To make the back cut, angle the saw slightly as you cut, forming a backward bevel.

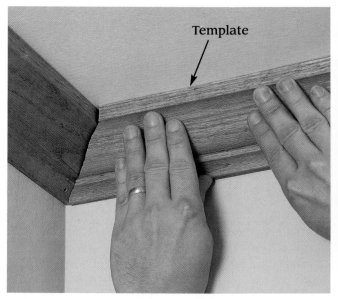

Template

7 Install the first piece of crown molding. Position the ends of the piece first, then push in the middle—it will snap into place, the ends digging into the walls slightly. Attach the trim by driving finish nails through pilot holes at wall stud locations. Set the nailheads with a nailset.

8 Rough-cut the next piece to length, allowing at least 6 in. extra for fitting the coped end. Before cutting the coped joint, place the appropriate coped and mitered template against the end of the first trim piece. If it fits tightly along the entire joint, cut the miter in the molding piece just as you did when making the template.

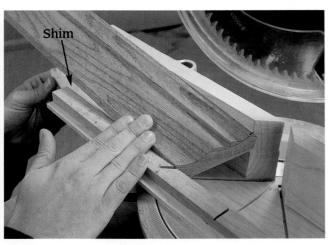

Shim

9 If there is a gap at the top of the template (step 8), measure its width. Position the new molding piece on the saw (upside-down) to cut a miter. Place a shim under the molding piece so the far end of the piece is raised. Use the shim to prop up the workpiece until the amount of lift at the cutting point equals the thickness of the gap at ceiling. Hold or clamp the workpiece securely and make the cut. Cut the cope with a coping saw. If there is a gap at the bottom of the template, follow the same procedure, except place the shim under the molding piece so the end nearer the blade is raised.

10 When the end of the second piece is cut and coped, test the fit. Make small adjustments with a wood rasp or sharp knife. If the edge of one piece is slightly proud of the other, it is best to bring it flush with a file or sandpaper, rather than re-cutting. If the walls aren't square, you may need to shim behind the molding at the wall. Butt the coped piece against the first piece in the corner, mark the other end and cut it to the correct length. Then install (unless the other end falls at an outside corner—see steps 11 to 14).

11 After cutting the opposite end, position the first workpiece at an outside corner (the reference lines on the ceiling should already be marked—See step 4). Mark the top and bottom of the cut you'll need to make on the face of the workpiece.

12 Make a test miter cut on the workpiece a couple of inches outside the top and bottom reference marks made in step 11. Measure from the reference line to the cut end. If the measurements are equal, make the same cut at the reference line. If not, adjust the saw set-up as needed.

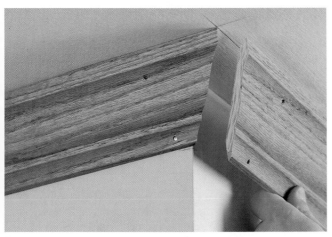

13 Install the mating piece of the outside corner. Apply glue to the mating ends to help hold the joint together.

14 After the glue dries, clean up any small mismatches in the joint with a rasp or file.

15 If shorter pieces of molding must be spliced together (avoid this situation as best you can), cut a scarf joint to make the splice. Position and cut a 45° bevel at the scarf joint end of one piece, so the cut angles away from the piece. Make a complementary 45° cut in the mating piece. Position the pieces against the ceiling and wall and test the fit. Make adjustments with a wood rasp or sharp knife. When the joint fits well, attach the molding piece that forms the bottom of the scarf joint first.

TIP: *Visible gaps between the top of the crown molding and the ceiling can be reduced simply by applying joint compound to the ceiling to fill the gap. Feather the compound gradually to avoid the appearance of ridges and swells. Mask the molding to protect it from the compound.*

Prefabricated miterless moldings

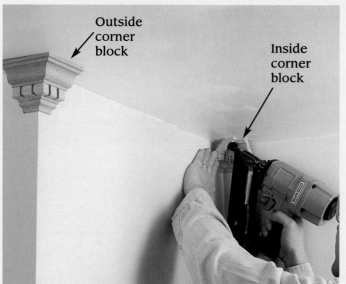

Outside corner block

Inside corner block

An easy installation of complicated cornices and crown moldings is possible with a product available from a few manufacturers. Instead of mitering or coping joints, you purchase preformed inside and outside corner pieces (left photo). You install these first, then cut molding—available in variable lengths, depending on the manufacturer—to fit with butt joints (although a little back-cutting of the molding piece ensures a tight fit). Simply fit the molding between the corner blocks (right photo) If the molding is too short, rather than making a scarf joint for splicing molding lengths together, plinth blocks are placed between butt joints. A fairly wide range of styles is available.

VARIATION:
Crown molding backing

A successful ceiling molding installation requires solid nailing surfaces in the ceiling behind the molding. Where the wall is perpendicular to the ceiling joists, the joists serve as adequate nailing surfaces. But walls running parallel to the ceiling joists pose a problem. To create a nailing surface in these situations, you can either install a backer that spans from cap plate to cap plate on opposing stud walls (right photo). Or, attach beveled nailing strips to the existing top plate at the wall/ceiling intersection (bottom photos).

2 × 6 backer

Top plate

Open-joist ceiling: In new construction, or where the ceiling surface has been removed, it is relatively simple to attach a 2 × 6 backer to the top plates of the stud walls.

Retrofit construction: Attach backer strips to the ceiling and wall surfaces. Mark the position of the molding on the ceiling and wall. Rip ¾-in. plywood strips that will butt up to the backside of the molding. The strip against the ceiling should butt against the wall and will be installed first. One edge of each strip is beveled to match the angle of the molding. This is usually 45° to vertical, but some moldings may be 35° or 32°. NOTE: Rip and cut the bevels for these strips on a table saw. Use a push stick when cutting these thin strips. Hold the ceiling strip in place (you will need a helper), then position the wall strip tightly against the ceiling strip before attaching the wall strip to wall studs with screws long enough to penetrate the studs 1½ in. Then drive screws into the corner between the two strips to secure the ceiling strip (top photo).

Index

Index of manufacturers

Abbingdon Affiliates, Inc.
(Metal ceilings)
Brooklyn, NY, (718) 258-8333

American Olean
(Flooring & wall tile)
Dallas, TX, (888) AOT-TILE;
www.aotile.com

Chelsea Decorative Metal Co.
(Metal ceilings)
Houston, TX, (713) 721-9200;
www.thetinman.com

Congoleum Corp.
(Resilient flooring)
Mercerville, NJ, (800) 274-3266;
www.congoleum.com

Dal-Tile
(Flooring & wall tile,
isolation membrane)
Dallas, TX, (800) 933-TILE;
www.daltile.com

Glidden Co.
(Paint)
Cleveland, OH, (800) GLIDDEN;
www.gliddenpaint.com

Historic Floors of Oshkosh
(Hardwood flooring,
decorative inlays)
Winneconne, WI, (920) 582-9977

Mannington Mills, Inc.
(Laminate & resilient flooring)
Salem, NJ, (800) 443-5667;
www.mannington.com

Norske Skog Flooring
(Laminate flooring)
Racine, WI, (414) 632-7583;
www.alloc.com

Shanker Industries
(Metal panel ceilings)
Oceanside, NY, (516) 766-4477

Specification Chemicals
(Nu-Wal, p. 132)
(Plaster repair membrane)
Macedonia, OH, (800) 247-3932;
www.specchem.com

USG Corp.
(Acoustical ceilings)
Chicago, IL, (800) USG-4YOU;
www.USG.com